Economic Development Strategies for State and Local Governments

Economic Development Strategies for State and Local Governments

Editors

Robert P. McGowan
University of Denver

Edward J. Ottensmeyer
Clark University

Nelson-Hall Publishers/Chicago

Library of Congress Cataloging-in-Publication Data

Economic development strategies for state and local governments /
  edited by Robert P. McGowan and Edward J. Ottensmeyer.
    p.   cm.
  Includes bibliographical references and index.
  ISBN 0-8304-1298-0
  1. Economic development projects—United States. 2. United
States—Economic policy—1981– 3. Local government—United States.
4. State governments.   I. McGowan, Robert P. II. Ottensmeyer,
Edward J. (Edward Joseph), 1946–
HC110.E44E25   1993   92-38093
338.973–dc20   CIP

Manufactured in the United States of America

10 9 8 7 6 5 4 3 2 1

™ The paper used in this book meets the
minimum requirements of American
National Standard for Information
Sciences—Permanence of Paper for
Printed Library Materials, ANSI
Z39.48-1984.

To Nancy and Anne

Contents

ACKNOWLEDGMENTS

IN PREPARING material for this book—an undertaking that was over two years in the doing—we have enjoyed the consistent and enthusiastic support of Stu Nagel of the Policy Studies Organization, of Dean Bruce Hutton (Denver) and Dean Robert Ullrich (Clark), and of the editorial staff at Nelson-Hall. Without their help this volume would not have been possible.

A talented and understanding group of authors made our work especially enjoyable from start to finish. We have them to thank for the many fresh ideas and insights that reside in this volume.

PART ONE

Introduction

ONE

EMERGING ISSUES IN ECONOMIC DEVELOPMENT

Robert P. McGowan and Edward J. Ottensmeyer

IN A recent report, the Corporation for Enterprise Development stated that the fifty states, along with the developed nations of the world, are in a race for the economic future—a race for leadership and dominance in a global economic marketplace (Corporation for Enterprise Development, 1988). Running in this race may mean developing high technology research parks to facilitate the flow of new ideas and innovation, starting business incubators to provide low rent and management support to start-up firms, promoting export of local products to international markets, or providing various incentives to attract expanding firms. In addition, there is concern on the part of all race-runners about the growing mismatch between emerging jobs, which will require new skills, and the skills of the people now available to fill them. Critical skill shortages may result when twenty-first century jobs intersect an aging U.S. workforce. The uncertainties of the new job market will be most troubling for people already at work. Tomorrow's careers will entail a lifelong commitment to retraining and the prospect of frequent, short bouts of unemployment.

In order to meet such challenges, a number of state and local governments have been making conscious, incremental investments in their ability to support and assist businesses in the challenge of economic development. According to the Corporation for Enterprise Development, successful states have recognized that economic development is a multifaceted, long term investment which involves a variety of activities to address a multitude of outcomes.

The purpose of this book is to examine the role of economic development from multiple perspectives—in particular, we focus on economic development strategies at the state and local level. While a great deal of research and writing has been undertaken that has examined economic development from a single state or local perspective, the body of work that has addressed common issues in state and local economic development is still emerging (Beaumont and Hovey, 1985; Grady, 1987; Steinnes, 1984). Yet, one factor that continually stands out in analyses of economic development is the critical role of investment in both physical and human capital—broadly defined. In this book, specific relationships between such investments and economic development outcomes are examined systematically.

Economic Development Defined

Economic development is a difficult concept to define. Almost every observer has his or her own favorite definition—ranging from attracting new businesses to developing centers of research excellence. In addition, economic development has become the darling of nearly every politician. Several states have elevated economic development work to cabinet status; numerous public-private task forces have been constituted to recommend ways to enhance or turn around state or local economic fortunes.

A report by the National Alliance of Business best describes the role of economic development: Economic development programs attempt to influence business investment in order to produce jobs, personal income, public revenues, and physical redevelopment (National Alliance of Business, 1987). In an earlier era, the economic development game was played with land write-downs, industrial parks, tax breaks, and advertising. The strategy was business attraction—mainly targeted at major manufacturers. In recent years, small business incubators, enterprise zones, specialized high-tech parks, export promotion, and focused equity funds have been added to the array of policy instruments. Business attraction is now balanced with retention and expansion of existing businesses; and the practice of economic development has expanded, diversified, and grown more sophisticated.

Perhaps the simplest manner in which to define economic development is by the outcomes that are expected to result from development activity. It is agreed that successful economic development strategies will lead to the following:

- job creation and retention
- tax revenue growth
- improved quality of life
- enhanced innovation/competitiveness

Job creation and retention is a basic measure used to illustrate the extent to which the benefits of economic activity are shared. Individuals gauge the performance of an economy by whether they have a job or not (Corporation for Enterprise Development, 1988). In any state, jobs are continually being created and eliminated. The more energetic and flexible the economy, the more this is the case. Job growth does not tell us whether jobs being created pay as well as those being eliminated, who is getting the new jobs, or whether employment growth is simply a reflection of population growth. It simply tells us how quickly an economy is expanding.

The second outcome, *tax revenue growth,* is closely linked to the previous outcome. Obviously, states stand to benefit directly from those businesses that choose to locate or stay. This translates into both corporate and individual taxes collected. At the same time, there are certain characteristics of a tax system that need to be considered by public officials. These would include the need for a balanced tax system that does not unduly burden one particular segment or group. In addition, the stability of tax systems is often used to provide businesses with the assurances they need to justify long-term investments.

The third area, *improved quality of life,* is perhaps the most difficult to articulate in terms of economic development outcomes. The implicit assumption here is that economic development—if done correctly—does not necessarily result in sacrificing the environment. Seeking this outcome has generated a mad dash by states to attract and retain "clean industries," such as advanced technology firms, which are seen to pollute the environment less and to employ a more educated workforce than heavy manufacturing industries. Another example of a clean industry is the service enterprise. Yet states tend to be somewhat hesitant here since these firms pay lower wages, can relocate quickly, and conduct business based on economies of scale.

The fourth outcome, *enhanced innovation and competitiveness,* is one that is increasingly emphasized. A recent work by the Conference Board defined "competitiveness" as "the degree to which a nation, under free and fair market conditions, produces goods and services that meet the test of international markets while simultaneously maintaining and expanding the real income of its citizens" (Morrison et al., 1988). Considered at the state and local level, a critical determinant is often a strong research-oriented education base.

Economic Development Activities

A common thread that emerges in analysis of economic development is diversification in state and local economies. Through this mechanism, an area is not at the mercy of a few industrial sectors—witness the effects in the northwestern states of the downturn in both aerospace and lumber. States and cities attempt to address this issue by building a mix of cyclical, countercyclical, and recession-proof industries.

Four areas of high priority in the economic development strategies of states and localities are:

- manufacturing modernization
- high technology development
- new business creation
- service sector expansion

Economic development approaches in each of these areas have undergone a transformation in recent years, part of which has been the development of explicit links between human development and economic development.

Manufacturing Modernization

Not many years ago, economic development programs that focused on manufacturing were directed principally, if not exclusively, to attracting new industries to a specific area. Plant closings were viewed as random events, and the dislocated workers were dealt with after the fact. Today, states and localities that are heavily dependent on the manufacturing sector recognize that they cannot and should not block changes necessary to make the manufacturing sector stronger and more competitive. In fact, pro-active approaches by governments to develop alliances between manufacturing firms and the engineering or business schools of area universities are on the rise.

High-Technology Development

After a wave of high-tech euphoria, most places have determined that they are not likely to be the next Silicon Valley and have devoted their energies to adjusting to or taking advantage of opportunities generated by earlier high-technology developments. This has resulted in a variety of programs, including the formation of high-technology councils, the creation of high-technology parks, industry-university arrangements for technology commercialization, and measures for strengthening the science and technology curricula of colleges and universities.

The Office of Technology Assessment notes that state and local governments are attracted to high-technology industries because of this sector's rapid expansion and its presumed job-creation potential (U.S.

Office of Technology Assessment, 1984). High-technology industries are viewed as potential major forces in the revival of distressed areas and are assumed to be a key source of innovative ideas, products, and processes essential to modernizing older industries and maintaining competitiveness. On the other hand, critics argue that high-technology job projections are often unrealistically high, and that the sector's potential for reviving distressed areas has been overstated. In addition, some analysts see any ill-conceived move to get on the already damaged high-technology bandwagon as a needless diversion from the real work of putting in place the policies and programs vital to a state's or city's economic future.

New Business Creation

Business creation, in recent years, has become a central theme of economic development. The realization that small businesses account for a disproportionately large share of new jobs has prompted a variety of innovative approaches for stimulating new businesses and expanding existing ones. The focus in a number of states is to create a climate conducive to innovation and entrepreneurship. Programs to identify and nurture entrepreneurship are now widespread. They include: debt and equity capital financing; management assistance; mechanisms for linking inventors with entrepreneurs; and low-cost space and business services. Small and new businesses find it very difficult to afford even simple training. Thus, creative mechanisms for training entrepreneurs often provide them with the support that helps create new jobs.

Service Sector Expansion

The relationship between the service sector and economic development is not clearly defined or understood. This sector is an important component of the contemporary economic scene; increasing service sector productivity has become critical to the nation's long-term economic prospects.

The challenges in the service sector are many. Training and retraining programs must be designed to respond to the specialized needs of this sector. Employers need to realize the importance of regular skills-upgrading and retraining for service sector employees. The lack of transferability of skills due to specialized training within sectors is a significant one for service employees. Finally, it should be recognized that the growth of the service sector is not the answer to economic and labor force problems. Instead, it is a broad category of opportunity that has a range of skills, pay rates, and declining segments associated with it.

In sum, economic development activities can not be viewed in isolation. What happens in one sector or area can have an effect on another.
The wide variety of outcomes sought by, as well as the wide range of
activities stemming from, the economic development efforts of state and
local government units, underscores the impossibility of fully summariz-
ing where things stand in the United States in the early 1990s. What
we can do—and what we have attempted to do in this volume—is to
consider the overall topic through the eyes of several highly regarded
experts on different facets of the theory and practice of economic development. By exposing interested readers—economic development planners
and policy analysts, state and local political officials, business leaders,
academic specialists—to a carefully chosen sample of papers, we hope
to stimulate in them further analysis, reflection, and creativity as they
pursue the critical work lying ahead.

Organization and Overview

This book is organized into two major sections. The first examines economic development issues primarily from the state-level perspective. The
second focuses primarily on the local context of economic development.
However, given that state and local economic development efforts are often
connected in complex ways, the careful reader should not be surprised
to find some discussion of "local" in the "state" papers, and vice versa.

Six papers make up the section on state-level economic development
strategy. The first paper, by David Coursey and Barry Bozeman, examines
university-industry cooperative research and development within the
context of recent state and federal policy. Drawing upon survey research,
the authors develop a profile of university-industry R&D linkages based
on the pervasiveness, general characteristics, motivations, and benefits
to the cooperating parties. They conclude with a set of managerial implications and a call for creative problem solving on the part of state policy
makers interested in technology-based economic development programs.

The next three papers focus on different dimensions of export promotion. Rodney Erickson, noting that the relationship between exporting and state economic growth is fundamentally an ambiguous one,
begins by examining the difficulties in getting good data on state exports.
He also analyzes characteristics of the export promotion programs of
states, puts forward an agenda for future research, and offers his ideas
on the effectiveness of certain state programs. Throughout the paper,
Erickson emphasizes how important clear-headed analysis can be to
policy makers, as well as the pitfalls of merely "following the leader."

Ruth Grubel's paper provides an in-depth look at state trade offices
in Japan. Grubel documents a pattern of growing state involvement in

U.S. trade relations, and uses survey data on state trade offices in Japan to demonstrate how states are "truly becoming international actors in their own rights." On a very practical note, Grubel ends her analysis with a set of provocative questions for public policy makers to use in selecting an appropriate level of investment in foreign trade offices. Stephen Archer and Steven Maser, in the following paper, use data from the 1980s to carry out a two-stage analysis of the factors that might explain state-level export promotion budgets. They support Erickson's contention that our "conventional wisdom" about export promotion policies should be subjected to the harsh glare of systematic evaluation.

Scott Woodard provides an insider's look at recent economic development strategies in Colorado. In his case study, Woodard examines the intricacies of economic development policy formation within the political context, noting both pitfalls and success factors, and compares the Colorado experience to a strategic management model of the development process. Concluding the first section, David Sears, John Redman, Richard Gardner, and Stephen Adams examine the role of the states in rural economic development. They develop a number of critical questions, considerations, and suggestions for policymakers concerned with rural development issues.

Five papers focus on local-level economic development strategies. Three focus directly on the local contexts in which economic development strategies emerge, while two explore dimensions of firm location decisions. Richard Feiock and James Clingermayer begin the section with an exploration of the political-institutional environments in which local decisions take shape. They argue that these environments are often as critical as economic and demographic circumstances in explaining local economic development choices, and, further, that various configurations of these environmental forces result in differential abilities on the part of places to use certain policy instruments. In developing their argument, these authors describe the municipal reform movement and the skills needed to pursue particular development policies, and empirically test the relationship of form of local government to the adoption of five policy instruments.

While the first paper focuses primarily on the role of local government in economic development, Craig Humphrey and Rodney Erickson, in the second paper, call attention to the growing role of nonprofit local industrial development groups. These groups are examined in the context of two paradigms attracting increased attention from social scientists—the local dependence hypothesis and the growth machine hypothesis. Humphrey and Erickson, through their in-depth analyses of the players, the stakes, the costs, and the benefits involved in various local development policies, develop a set of fresh insights into the political-social-economic dimensions of local decision making.

Terry Buss and Roger Vaughan, using a case study format, document actions taken over a ten year period in response to the deindustrialization of Youngstown, Ohio. They describe federal, state, and local programs tried in an attempt to revitalize that manufacturing city, and explore why federal programs not only did not work but also hindered certain local programs, which have proven more effective. Based on their analyses of Youngstown and other communities, the authors develop several practical lessons for local decision makers.

William Waugh's paper examines in detail a key element of local economic development policy—transportation. He describes the perceived role of transportation in the site selection decisions of firms, and, using a survey of four U.S. industry groups, examines the relative emphasis placed on transportation by business decision makers. He then shifts perspective to discuss implications for local economic development strategy.

The final chapter, by Douglas Henderson, Stuart Hart, and Daniel Denison, represents a broad-gauged look at firm location decisions. The authors pose a deceptively simple research question: How do organizational differences influence a firm's preferences regarding location? The differences they then study are age, size, technology level, and industry. The authors trace the business location literature from its inception, point out its conceptual and methodological weaknesses, and summarize their own five year study of organizational influences on business location decisions. Their closing sections discuss business location decisions within a strategic planning perspective and explore ways in which local economic development planners might use these findings to better link the attributes of their communities to the decisions of firms.

As the above descriptions suggest, the chapters in this volume cover a wide range of topics from a variety of perspectives. Academic experts from business strategy, organizational behavior, economics, geography, political science, public administration, and sociology are joined by consultants, policy analysts, and economic development specialists to provide a perspective on economic development that is neither highly theoretical nor highly normative. Rather, we have sought to travel the middle—and, we hope, virtuous—road where the best of theory joins the best of policy analysis and practical experience to enhance both the understanding of academics interested in *studying* economic development issues and the effectiveness of those reflective practitioners actually *doing* the job.

PART TWO

State Government Issues and Economic Development

UNIVERSITY-INDUSTRY COOPERATIVE R&D: ISSUES AND ROLES IN STATE ECONOMIC DEVELOPMENT

David Coursey and Barry Bozeman

THE IVORY is being chiseled from the tower. During the past decade, increasing numbers of eager entrepreneurs and industrialists journeyed to universities in hopes of gathering nuggets of technology from which to develop or expand a business. Their hopes have been encouraged by a federal government increasingly promoting the commercialization of its research, long short on marketable products, towards economic competitiveness. Many state governments have followed the national government in supporting the commercial use of universities.

While there have been many recent changes in state economic development programs and services, policies enhancing university-industry cooperation are of particular concern. Universities cooperating with industry is hardly new, but the level of this activity and the states' increasing role in it is a fundamental change that many believe offers as much risk as potential economic benefit. Consider two exemplar incidents courtesy of the brave new world of university commercialism.

- *A Unique Tenure Story.* In Massachusetts, the state courts are considering the case of David Noble, a former MIT professor, who claims he was denied tenure for his outspoken opposition to increasing commercial activity at the university (Norman, 1990).
- *Shrinking Commitments.* Charter Medical Company announced in early 1990 that it was backing out of a deal under negotiation since 1987 with Stanford for a new $22 million psychiatry center that would have greatly improved the school's clinical base. The deal fell through, it is rumored, because of the company's losses when the junk bond market collapsed (Culliton, 1990).

Each of these stories represents some of the tribulations in university-industry cooperation. But, there are opportunities as well. Universities engaging in the business of technology development and transfer may expand their resource base, develop new research ideas and projects, enhance student placement, and most importantly to state economic development, contribute to the well-being of their state and region.

Our purpose is to provide state economic development practitioners some background on university-industry formal cooperative R&D, contractual arrangements by which the two jointly acquire technical knowledge (Link and Bauer, 1989). Certainly, there are other arrangements for university assistance to industry, but state and federal policymakers seek to formalize, institutionalize, and exploit fully arrangements between industry and universities. University-industry cooperative R&D may represent the greatest potential payoffs, problems, and risks among the myriad options facing economic development policymakers.

We begin by reviewing the forces behind the expanded university roles in economic development then turn to several open questions concerning university-industry cooperative R&D. What is the current level of joint activity? What are the characteristics of universities and industries involved in cooperative R&D? What are the motivations and perceived benefits of cooperation? Data from a recent survey of the U.S. research facilities is reported. From this analysis, we offer suggestions for state economic development policies.

Why the Push for University-Industry Cooperative R&D?

While universities and businesses, expecting varied benefits from their joint activities, have expanded cooperation on their own accord, a major push is from policymakers at the federal and state levels. The federal competitiveness rallying cry has yielded a variety of influential policy changes. At the state level, the catch phrase is regional economic development.

The Federal Push for University-Industry Cooperative R&Ds

In the last decade, federal promotion of technology transfer has greatly expanded. Most actions do not directly address university-industry relationships but instead overall cooperation among the nation's research labs. Through changes in antitrust regulations, tax credits, patent policy, new types of research centers, and research funding shifts, the federal government has attempted to improve the national economy through technological innovation resulting in commercializable products.

The bellwether of these changes was the Stevenson-Wydler Technological Innovation Act (1980) mandating that federal labs engage in technology transfer with industry, state governments, and universities. The act included numerous features supporing cooperative R&D with government labs but was vague concerning patent rights from joint activities (Rahm, 1989). Later in 1980, the Bayh-Dole Act permitted small businesses and nonprofit organizations to retain title to inventions they developed using federal funds either from cooperative agreements, contracts, or grants. The Uniform Patent and Procedures Act of 1983, the Trademark Clarification Act of 1984, and Federal Technology Transfer Act of 1986 expanded agency authority to grant patent rights and enumerated title policies. Prior to the passage of Bayh-Dole and its offspring, the federal government held title to all inventions from its funding which had the effect of slowing technology development by discouraging cooperative arrangements with government.

Towards special assistance for small businesses, the Small Business Innovation Development Act was passed in 1982 mandating that federal agencies with sizable R&D budgets form research programs facilitating the participation of small businesses in federal R&D. Tax credits were also included in the reform whirlwind. For example, the Economic Recovery and Tax Act of 1981 included tax incentives for industrial R&D and was particularly useful to university-industry cooperation because it eased certain restrictions enticing work at universities over government facilities. The cost-effectiveness of tax credits versus other policy options is questionable, especially given the cost in tax revenues (Bozeman and Link, 1984). A 1990 General Accounting Office study estimates the tax credit stimulated $1 billion to $2.5 billion of additional research spending at a cost of $7 billion in tax revenues between 1981 and 1985 ("the Research and Expenditure Tax Credit," 1990). One survey, mostly of vice presidents in charge of research for businesses and universities, found just over 30 percent believe the tax credit has increased cooperative activity (Fowler, 1984). Still, the Bush administration recently proposed making the tax credit permanent (Anthes, 1991).

Perhaps the most important legislative landmark for university-industry cooperative R&D is the 1984 National Cooperative Research Act. Before this act, firms engaged in cooperative research ventures risked potentially harsh antitrust prosecution. The legislation clarifies and extends Department of Justice decisions on R&D joint ventures permitting greater cooperation between businesses for research purposes. Businesses, simply by registering their joint activities with the federal government, greatly minimize the types of damages they could pay in antitrust actions.

The act's primary influence on university-industry cooperation is promoting joint business research often linked with universities. Since 1984, over 150 agreements have been filed, comprised of over 900 businesses and 200 government and university organizations (Smilor and Gibson, 1991). Some of these cooperative arrangements were formed before the relaxed antitrust guidelines,[1] but there is little doubt the expansion of activity is attributable to antitrust reform (Rahm, 1989).

Two years later the 1988 Omnibus Trade and Competitiveness Act made major changes in U.S. R&D policy giving the Department of Commerce primary responsibility for civilian technology development, creating an undersecretary of Commerce and forming the National Institute of Standards and Technology (NIST) from the old National Bureau of Standards (Jones, 1989). NIST is charged with research in a variety of areas supporting industrial innovation. Another critical feature is the Advanced Technology Program (ATP) assisting businesses in research and application of generic technologies, manufacturing techniques, and commercial products (Rahm, 1989), including proposals to fund high-definition television (HDTV) research (Rousch, 1990). Additionally, the act requires the president to submit an annual R&D policy statement and budget and calls for studies of cooperative R&D arrangements (Rahm, 1989).

Overall, this flurry of legislation represents a considerable government push for R&D cooperation. Besides legislation, numerous other events in federal R&D are significant influences. The continuing debate over the involvement of foreign firms in government supported R&D at universities, including Congressional inquiries of MIT's Industrial Liaison Program which includes a number of foreign firms (Gray, 1990), poses problems for academic freedom. Funding of university R&D is seen by many university researchers as seriously deficient encouraging investigators and the universities themselves to seek funding from cooperation with industry (cf. McHenry, 1990). The expansion of university-based research centers facilitating university-industry cooperation, sponsored by the National Science Foundation (NSF) and other federal agencies, in high-tech fields and interdisciplinary projects with strong commercial potential is another important event.

One of more significant developments is increased efforts by states, industries, and universities to circumvent peer review in project awards, namely pork-barrel R&D politics with its dangerous ramifications for the effectiveness of U.S. competitiveness efforts (for an overview, see Bozeman and Crow, in press). Efforts by states to attract big ticket projects such as the Superconducting Super Collider (SSC) have ushered a new era of competition for federal R&D dollars that in many ways is analogous to the "smoke stack" chasing of the 1970s. Elected officials argue federal R&D dollars are distributed unfairly and "high-tech pork" is justified on equity grounds. For example, 40 percent of federal dollars supporting industry research went to California in 1985 (Wolff, 1989).

NSF has responded to the new politics by dividing some research money for large projects, such as the SSC, among several states. Additionally, NSF's recent tendency to ask for matching funds in project awards constrains research universities which have less flexibility securing funds. The matching provides strong incentives for state involvement with university-industry proposals, especially expensive centers, while distracting state efforts from those smaller endeavors, such as improvements in science education, with arguably greater long-term payoffs.

The State Push for University-Industry Cooperative R&D

Until the 1980s, states did little to promote university-industry partnerships. However, with economic decline in major state industries and reduced domestic support during the Reagan era, numerous states either began or expanded programs supporting high-tech for economic development (Lambright and Teich, 1989). Before 1980 there were only nine state programs for technology development (Lambright and Rahm, 1990). By 1988, there were more than 500 state and local high-tech programs in forty-five states (Abelson, 1988), spending about $770 million a year, dwarfed by $58 billion in federal R&D expenditures (cf. Lambright and Rahm, 1990). State funds support diverse efforts including traditional industrial extension centers, educational programs, and university-based research centers for industry (for overviews, see Lambright and Teich, 1989; Jones, 1989; Lambright and Rahm, 1990; Minnesota DTED, 1988). These programs are managed under a variety of organizational arrangements. Some are assigned to agencies previously charged with economic development missions and some to completely new entities. Flexible organizational structures such as boards and foundations are common with the hope that the programs will be more responsive to change than traditional organizations.

In virtually all of the states deeply involved in technology-based economic development programs, universities play a central role in policy strategies. Almost 40 percent of the funding for these programs goes toward university activities (Jones, 1989). In New York, the state probably most involved with university-industry arrangements, the Science and Technology Foundation oversees a variety of programs, most significantly the Centers for Advanced Technology scattered across the state at seven universities and including Cornell's Center for Biotechnology in Agriculture and Syracuse University's Center for Computer Applications and Software Engineering. In 1987, the foundation funded 137 projects with $17.5 million in state money and $57.5 million in matching funds from federal and industry sources. Other strategies include infusing universities with more research funding, hoping increased capabilities will yield economic results, and establishing university research parks, banking on the importance of proximity in technology transfer success.

Questions in University-Industry Cooperative R&D

State and federal efforts push joint research activity in search of economic gain and pose important questions for public policymakers in the aftermath. We address a few of these questions using data from Part III of the National Comparative R&D Laboratory Project (NCRDP), a broad research effort in science and technology policy involving investigators at several universities including Syracuse, Iowa State, North Carolina, Virginia Tech, Florida State, and South Florida. Part III consists of a mail survey to over one thousand U.S. research laboratory directors concerning technology transfer, cooperative R&D, and other topics as a followup to a previous project phase funded by the National Science Foundation (Bozeman and Crow, 1988, 1990). Only the subset of industry and university laboratories were examined here (NCRDP data base also includes government and nonprofit laboratories). The 63 university lab responses are from a mailing of 164 (38 percent response rate); the 261 industry lab responses are from a mailing of 594 (41 percent response rate). The overall response rate for the 534 laboratories in the NCRDP database is 47 percent.

How Pervasive Is University-Industry Cooperative R&D?

Results suggest many university and industry labs are involved in cooperative R&D though much of that activity is located at a handful of labs and common indicators of university commercial success, such as fees received from patents and licenses, present little reason for optimism. Of the university labs sampled, 30 (46 percent) report formal cooperative R&D agreements with businesses. Results for the industrial labs are similar with 108 (42 percent) noting university agreements. While this suggests substantial participation, the actual number of agreements tempers this conclusion. Of the labs engaged in university-industry cooperative R&D, half the universities report less than three industrial agreements while half of the industrial labs indicate less than two university arrangements. More telling is the disparity in the number of agreements across labs. Two university labs are responsible for 65 percent of industrial agreements while just a couple of businesses hold 31 percent of the industry arrangements with colleges.

The sheer number of agreements is not a complete picture. Licenses, patents, copyrights, and the revenues generated from them, to some extent represent commercial success of universities in fostering economic development. The university labs involved in cooperative R&D with industry reported a total of forty-one licensed and ninety-four patented technologies during 1989, or less than two licenses and just over three patents per university lab. The average revenue from these licenses, patents, and copyrights is a lowly $3,382, with just two labs accounting for 77 percent of the total generated revenue of $71,021.

University-industry cooperative R&D exists in many places but activity is concentrated among a few institutions—the largest laboratories. The largest university lab in the sample, by total R&D budget ($150 million), total workforce (1,600), and total scientific and engineering personnel (900), is located at one of the nation's best research institutions and is responsible for over one-third of the reported university-industry formal agreements. The two industry labs controlling 31 percent of the university arrangements are also huge. One is in the top 5 percent of all three size measures, while the other is in the top 15 percent in R&D budget and roughly the top third in both personnel measures.

What Are the Characteristics of Cooperating Labs?

Do university and industry labs engaged in joint activity differ from other college and business research units? There are no significant differences in average total workforce or R&D budgets between universities engaged and not engaged in industrial cooperative R&D. Industry labs working with universities are larger than other firms. Labs cooperating with colleges on average have larger R&D budgets ($37 to $18 million) and much larger scientific workforces (284 to 118).

Both university groups rate basic research as equally important, but those working with industry place greater importance on applied and commercial research. College labs cooperating with firms devote a greater percentage of their total budget to applied (26 percent to 13 percent) and commercial research (7 percent to 3 percent) and proportionally less for basic science (40 percent to 66 percent). Industrial labs working with higher education devote more of their budgets to pre-commercial applied research (22 percent to 13 percent) than other business R&D facilities. They also view their missions as more orientated towards basic and pre-commercial applied research than industry labs not active in cooperative R&D.

The results suggest the industrial players are big labs with more pre-commercial research orientations than their competitors. Major corporations, perhaps due to their greater resources allowing for more pre-commercial research common in cooperative R&D with universities, are more involved than small companies. There is a perception that only large firms can afford formal cooperative arrangements with colleges that often involve substantial outlays and risk (McHenry, 1990) associated with the pre-commercial and basic research common in university agreements. Our findings support these perceptions. This is alarming if one accepts the view that small firms offer the best return for the economic development dollar. Lists of research partners in major university-based research centers suggest large firms are much more common players. However, many states try supporting small firms in joint research with universities. Pennsylvania's Ben Franklin Partnership encourages cooperation among firms of all size with university and government labs and includes seed money for the venture capital funds so critical to small businesses. Over half the twenty-five hundred firms working with the state's universities are small enterprises (Abelson, 1988). But, the general perception remains that the giants play with the universities.

In universities, differences in size do not appear major explanations for industrial efforts across all the institutions but yet the very top player is a large, prestige research school. This suggests university activity is concentrated at the top schools with many others perhaps just dabbling. Industrial funding at MIT has been growing at a rate of 20 percent per year since 1976 and as of 1987 totalled over $36 million, 15 percent of the university's budget. In 1987, Carnegie Mellon's industry support constituted 23 percent of its research budget with rapid growth expected (Biddle, 1987). Government policies favoring greater distribution of R&D dollars, from NSF matching funds with state governments to pork-barrel policies, are partially responses to this dominance some view as inequitable. The big university players devote more resources to applied and commercial research than other colleges signalling the growth of commercial campuses.

What Are the Motivations and Benefits?

Success stories of particular products or dollars of industrial funds flowing to university research are trumpeted as evidence of successful arrangements. Inference from such evidence is limited due to difficulties in specifying the economic effects of programs that have not been long in place.

Advocates of university-industry cooperation enumerate not only economic benefits for the population, but also payoffs to the individual partners. After all, universities and businesses cannot be realistically expected to cooperate without at least some foreseeable payoff. In our survey of laboratory directors, we asked those engaged in cooperative R&D to assess several possible motives. Table 2.1 gives the results dividing the university respondents by whether each item was at least somewhat a motivation versus very little or not at all. Table 2.2 provides the industry findings.

Table 2.1   Motivations for Cooperative R&D: University Labs with Formal Agreements with Industry

	Great deal/ Somewhat	Very little/ Not at all
Fundamental scientific knowledge	23 (82%)	5 (18%)
New technology or applied knowledge	25 (89%)	3 (11%)
Contribute to other parties in the agreement	16 (57%)	12 (43%)
Incentives provided by other parties in agreement	14 (50%)	14 (50%)
Incentives provided by the National Cooperative Research Act of 1984	0 (0%)	27 (100%)
Personnel exchange opportunities	9 (32%)	19 (68%)
Increased profits/resources for lab or parent organizations	19 (68%)	9 (32%)

Table 2.2   Motivations for Cooperative R&D: Industry Labs with Formal Agreements with Universities

	Great deal/ Somewhat	Very little/ Not at all
Fundamental scientific knowledge	48 (48%)	51 (52%)
New technology or applied knowledge	91 (89%)	11 (11%)
Contribute to other parties in the agreement	41 (42%)	57 (58%)
Incentives provided by other parties in agreement	39 (41%)	57 (59%)
Incentives provided by the National Cooperative Research Act of 1984	6 (6%)	89 (94%)
Personnel exchange opportunities	27 (28%)	69 (72%)
Increased profits/resources for lab or parent organizations	75 (76%)	24 (24%)

The findings suggest the two groups share many of the same motivations. University labs are significantly higher, based on appropriate statistical tests,[2] on only two motivations: desire for fundamental scientific knowledge and contribution to the other parties in the agreement. Profit is more important to industry but the difference is not significant.

The lack of difference on some items is also intriguing. We expected industry to be more motivated by the National Cooperative Research Act of 1984 and, while we did not expect the act was a powerful motivation, the extremely low importance indicated by respondents is troubling. Does this mean the incentives provided by the act are ineffectual? There are reasons for avoiding this conclusion. Additional analysis found a positive association between the number of university cooperative R&D agreements held by industry labs and the appeal of the incentives provided by the act ($r=.16$; $p<.10$). This seems to suggests the act is more important in encouraging joint R&D in labs already experienced in cooperative relations than in prompting newcomers. Finally, the nearly identical importance placed on new technology and applied knowledge suggests the nature of these agreements, as is strongly evidenced by the case study literature, is for more applied work.

Besides motivations, do the labs perceive similar benefits? It might be expected that universities improve their basic research effectiveness while industrial labs promote their commercial and applied research. Table 2.3 contains the results of an item asking respondents involved in university-industry agreements how cooperative R&D agreements in general are improving their basic, applied, and commercial research effectiveness. A great majority of the universities perceive cooperative R&D

Table 2.3   Cooperative R&D Benefits in Improving Research Effectiveness: Universities and Industries

	Great deal/ Somewhat	Very little/ Not at all
Industry Labs		
Basic research	65 (65%)	36 (36%)
Precommercial applied research	80 (78%)	23 (22%)
Commercial applied research and development	74 (72%)	29 (28%)
University Labs		
Basic research	24 (86%)	4 (14%)
Precommercial applied research	18 (64%)	10 (36%)
Commercial applied research and development	11 (31%)	17 (69%)

improving their usual speciality, basic research. Industries note improvements in commercial and precommercial work. The benefits vary, but the confidence that cooperative R&D supports the typical research mission of these two types of labs is encouraging, since these formal arrangements appear mutually beneficial in improving capabilities in varied research.

Interesting results are also found comparing labs within each of the two groups. For example, industry labs active in cooperative R&D can be separated into those that do and those that do not have joint activity with universities. This acts as a control for cooperative arrangements with government and other labs. Statistical tests indicate industry labs engaged in university arrangements are more motivated by basic research needs (56 percent to 20 percent) and that they see greater benefits in their basic research capabilities (70 percent to 40 percent) than industry labs involved with other cooperative R&D partners such as government or other firms. University labs with industrial R&D partners are more motivated by applied research (91 percent to 62 percent) compared to college labs cooperating with other universities or government. There are other notable percentage differences in the two university groups but the college sample size (thirty labs) is too small to conclude they are reliable findings. For example, the universities engaged in joint R&D with industrial labs indicated greater benefit in their applied research (68 percent to 38 percent) and technology transfer efforts (50 percent to 25 percent) as well as greater motivation for incentives provided by their R&D partners (54 percent to 25 percent).

Implications for Practice

The survey results have important implications in shaping state economic development policies banking on university-industry cooperative R&D. It appears many university and industry labs are cooperating but only a few are mounting substantial efforts. This may be more a reflection of the newness of cooperative efforts than failing state and federal policies. Large firms placing greater importance on pre-commercial research are the common industry players. However, though much university activity flows from the largest laboratory, size does not generally appear a major factor for universities. Size may be more important for industry, because it reflects slack resources necessary for the more risky, long-term nature of precommercial research, while universities commonly serve basic and sometimes applied scientific objectives. More importantly for planning, this suggests the size of the university is not a critical factor. Geographic proximity may be more important. Proximity is considered one of the major reasons for one of the oldest and largest cooperative arrangements, that between Monsanto and Washington University in St. Louis, and the failure of the company's work with the larger, more distant Harvard University (cf. Culliton, 1990; McHenry, 1990).

Differences in university and industry motivations and benefits are also concerning to policymakers attempting to marry seemingly estranged research perspectives. The findings indicate cooperating universities and industries are quite similar. Universities do have greater basic research motivations but they have surprisingly strong commitment to more applied research and to helping their research partners. This is especially true compared to universities involved with nonindustrial partners.

Industries working with universities are more prone to precommercial research than firms cooperating with other lab owners. This suggests the two cultures maintain their typical perspectives but meet each other in a mutually beneficial middle-ground between basic research and short-term, low-risk research—exactly the role many planners envision for these arrangements.

The emerging picture is hopeful with differences in motivations hardly as drastic as many believe. However, it should be noted the data concern those *involved* in cooperative R&D. It is quite likely those not involved in cooperative R&D retain such opposing motivations that promoting their cooperation will prove challenging. In some cases, such as with small firms, states may wish to exert special efforts. However, it is quite possible states will achieve greater payoffs encouraging the efforts of cooperative institutions rather than soliciting cooperative R&D from the reluctant.

There are other state challenges. One is not overemphasizing the commercial role of universities which play an essential educational role critical to long-term economic success. Growing linkages may foster more opportunities for students and help improve the alarming deterioration of college research facilities, but they may also distract from educational objectives (Gander, 1986). States must work in cooperation with the federal government and other states as well. The National Governor's Association maintains a R&D working group towards improving communication and cooperation between states and the national government (Jones, 1989). As "laboratories of democracy," states can experiment more with alternative arrangements and policies (Osborne, 1988).

There is no template for building successful university-industry arrangements; policymakers should be creative, experimental, and informed. The need for flexibility questions devoting most resources into a few large projects, exemplified by supporting large university research centers. States may be too enamored of large projects and too hasty in chasing costly federal research centers. For example, Florida recently bankrolled $58 million in landing a $118 million national magnetics laboratory from the NSF (Hamilton, 1990). Once the fanfare over beating MIT for the project has subsided, Florida, and other states devoting large outlays to centers, must ask themselves if the money could have been used more effectively in smaller projects with perhaps more certain economic payoffs.

Notes

1. For example, the Gas Research Institute, the Electric Power Research Institution (EPRI), and the National Science Foundation's Industry/University Cooperative Research Centers program were all formed in the 1970s. In fact, another early and prominent consortium, the Microelectronic and Computer Technology Corporation (MCC) was instrumental in the development of antitrust reform (Evan and Olk, 1990).
2. Difference in mean t-tests and Mann-Whitney U tests (suitable for ordinal data and nonnormal interval distributions) are used where appropriate in judging statistical significance throughout this paper. Net differences were judged statistically significant if there was less than a one in ten chance they could be obtained in a random sample when the two groups were exactly equal across all the labs.

THREE

TRADE, ECONOMIC GROWTH, AND STATE EXPORT PROMOTION PROGRAMS

Rodney A. Erickson

THE U.S. economy has become much more integrated into the global economy during the latter part of the twentieth century than ever before. In 1970, U.S. merchandise exports totalled $42.7 billion, an amount equal to 4.2 percent of gross national product (GNP) (U.S. Bureau of the Census, 1990: 425, 804). By 1990, merchandise exports had increased to $397.9 billion, a real (inflation-adjusted) increase of 239 percent over the 1970 level, and equal to 7.3 percent of GNP (U.S. Bureau of Economic Analysis, 1991: 8, 15, 23).

Unfortunately, the propensity of U.S. consumers and businesses to import has grown even more rapidly. Since 1970, the national economy has experienced a merchandise trade surplus in only three years (1970, 1973, and 1975). Trade deficits soared by the mid-1980s to more than $100 billion annually, reaching a peak of nearly $160 billion in 1987. Much of this deficit can be attributed to a shrinking trade surplus in agricultural commodities coupled with substantial trade deficits in petroleum, motor vehicles, and general industrial, telecommunications, and electrical equipment.

These persistently high trade deficits have elicited widespread calls from government and industry leaders to bolster existing approaches and create new ones to curb imports while stimulating exports. Proposed remedies have taken the form of legislation to limit imports through quotas and tariffs, stricter enforcement of antidumping agreements, and various programs to encourage sales in foreign markets. The Omnibus Trade and Competitiveness Act of 1988 [PL 100-418] targets the resources of various federal agencies and programs into a coordinated effort to stimulate exporting among U.S. firms. Both the Reagan and Bush

Administrations have pushed freer trade within North America and else-where, seeking to break down barriers to U.S. goods and services in for-eign markets. The recent round of GATT (General Agreement on Tariffs and Trade) talks also reflect a resolve to create what U.S. trade negotia-tors call "a more level playing field" for export firms.

The importance of exporting in the trade equation is further documented in recent research by Hanink (1987) that draws on previ-ous studies by Armington (1969) and Norman (1986). Hanink argues and provides indirect evidence from U.S., West German, and Japanese trade data to support the proposition that the current American trade deficit is primarily due to the inability of American firms to export well, rather than the United States being an import market easily penetrated by com-peting foreign firms.

State and local governments have also become increasingly interested in export promotion activities. This rush to stimulate exports is evidenced in the substantial increases in state budgetary commitments to inter-national programs over the past decade (Berry and Mussen, 1980; National Association of State Development Agencies [NASDA], 1984; 1986; 1988; 1991). These programs cover a wide range of activities includ-ing information services, marketing, substate and interstate cooperation, export finance, training programs, and regulatory change (Archer and Maser, 1989). To date, there has been a paucity of research evaluting the impact of state export promotion programs. While the conceptual and methodological impediments to an evaluation of state export programs are alone substantial, an even more serious problem arises from the lack of suitable state trade data.

The purpose of this chapter is to provide a critical assessment of research concerning the role of export trade in state economic growth, the data and other limitations to such analyses, the characteristics of state export promotion programs, and some preliminary thoughts on the potential effectiveness of certain types of state export programs. The chap-ter concludes with an agenda outlining the needs for future research.

Data Limitations in State Export Activity Analysis

The principal sources for state trade data are the Foreign Trade Division (FTD) and the Industry Division (ID) of the U.S. Bureau of the Census. These two divisions, however, publish different state trade data drawn from different sources, both with their particular strengths and limita-tions (Farrell and Radspieler, 1989). The Bureau of the Census has made the former data available on an annual and quarterly basis since 1987 with only a few months time lag. The latter annual data have been pub-lished over the past three decades with some missing years. There is typically a two to three year time lag in obtaining these ID state export data.

The Foreign Trade Division provides export data based upon the U.S. Customs Service declarations of domestic exporter firms. These data are extensive and relatively complete records of U.S. export trade with foreign countries (except for estimated small transactions with Canada and, of course, what smuggling takes place). These value of shipments export data are available for combinations of state, foreign destinations, and two-digit Standard Industrial Classification (SIC) code. At the national level, the data are considered to be highly reliable for individual SIC categories; the data are also very reliable for (first) foreign destination, although no account can be made of U.S. exports to foreign transshipment points that are then reexported to other, ultimate destinations. Serious problems arise, however, with the attribution of exports to their source states of production in the United States. The declaration form completed by the exporter asks for the origin of the shipment, but a significant problem exists when goods are produced in one state, perhaps processed further in another, and packaged or otherwise brokered at the port which may be in a third state. The pattern of state exports is inherently biased toward those states with major ports. This problem is particularly acute in the case of relatively undifferentiated commodity exports such as cereal grains, coal, or timber. For example, Louisiana would appear in the FTD data to be the major state of production of exported wheat when, in reality, it is the "point of shipment consolidation" of these undifferentiated goods. These data are based on f.a.s. (free alongside ship) values and therefore include the various wholesale and transportation costs that accrue beyond the point of production. Finally, a substantial share of the shipments (21.5 percent for the manufacturing sector alone in 1987 based on this author's calculations) cannot be attributed to a particular state based on information from the shipper's export declaration.

Thus, while the FTD data are a rich source of information on state export flows and are reliable with respect to SICs and destinations, they are inherently flawed for tracking state-level exports. Unfortunately, many state officials used these data as though the exports attributed to their state were actually produced there. Some analysts combined these exports data with state imports data from the Bureau of the Census's FT990 publication, *Highlights of U.S. Export and Import Trade*, to create state foreign trade balances. However, imports are allocated to particular states based on the address of the consignee, and the data are therefore heavily biased toward those states with concentrations of corporate headquarters rather than the state in which the goods actually enter the domestic market. A state trade balance is inherently flawed conceptually and, in any case, it is difficult to imagine what such a measure would tell an analyst or policymaker.

The data on state exports provided by the Industry Division is based upon the share of value of shipments destined for export markets (sold directly or through brokers) as reported by manufacturing establishments annually. The *Census of Manufactures* (CM) provides a complete reporting of establishments on five-year cycle; intervening years are covered in the *Annual Survey of Manufactures* (ASM). These data provide information on value of export shipments f.o.b. (freight on board) at the place of production. Export employment is derived from the share of exports in the total value of the establishment's shipments. In addition, indirect exports (those goods and services required as intermediate inputs in the production of the direct exports) are estimated for individual states by the U.S. Bureau of Economic Analysis using an input-output modeling procedure with allocations of indirect requirements to the various states. Although these data are clearly the most accurate for exports by state of production, the substantial time lag in their availability and lack of coverage for the nonmanufacturing sectors limits their usefulness for state-level analysis. Unfortunately, recent research involving the merger of the FTD and ID data sets on exports has not yet disaggregated the resulting industrial export flows data beyond nine multistate regions in the United States (Erickson and Hayward, 1991a).

Thus, the lack of a completely suitable set of state (or local) data on exports has limited the types of trade analysis that can be appropriately undertaken. The Exporter Data Base (EDB), currently being developed at the Bureau of the Census, should eventually provide state and metropolitan export and import data and the characteristics of establishments and firms engaged in trade. This will be accomplished by linking the shipper's export declaration to Census establishment records. However, state exports from service businesses and those that produce undifferentiated commodity exports provide their own unique problems that will be very difficult to overcome.

Interstate Variations in Relative Export Performance

Empirical analysis indicates that substantial interstate variation exists in relative export performance. Using 1986 ASM data, Erickson and Hayward (1991b) have shown that total industrial exports (direct plus indirect) as a percent of total value of shipments range from 7.7 percent in Wyoming to 28.3 percent in Washington, with a median of 12.4 percent. States located in coastal or border areas are generally characterized by a higher proportion of their industrial production destined for export markets.

Interstate variations in relative export performance are closely related to differences in the industry structures of the states. Those states whose industries include sectors that are characterized nationally by strong export performances are obviously better positioned to be successful exporters. The ASM data for 1986 reveal a wide variation among three-digit SIC manufacturing industries in terms of the total shares of their output that are directly or indirectly exported (Erickson and Hayward, 1991b). The highest export share in an industry with significant output occurs in the electronic components and accessories industry (SIC 367) with 51.1 percent of its output exported directly or indirectly. Other high export industries include certain chemicals, electrical and nonelectrical machinery, transportation equipment, and metals industries. In contrast, the lowest ranking export sectors include such predominantly domestic market producers as food products, apparel, and building materials (e.g., stone, paving materials, flooring, and millwork).

Numerous authors have noted that state industrial export composition, mirroring the national pattern, tends to embody relatively high levels of capital, both physical and human (Gillespie, 1982; Feileke, 1986; Erickson and Hayward, 1991b). Coughlin and Cartwright (1987a) have shown that the total volume of state industrial exports is significantly related to the respective states' endowments of manufacturing capital and skilled labor. In a more detailed analysis, Erickson and Hayward (1991b) found that the relative export efficiency of industries (defined as the state's share of exports of an industry relative to its share of total shipments for all industries) was significantly related to the capital intensity of the various sectors in 39 of the 48 contiguous states. The parameters from these regressions were subsequently related to the factor endowments across the various states. While factor endowments accounted for only a limited share of interstate variation in relative export performance, physical and human capital in manufacturing were shown to be significant explanatory variables.

Exports and State Economic Growth

The relationship between exporting and state economic growth is really an ambiguous one, although much of the general public and many state policymakers seem to regard it as an axiomatic one. This presumption probably stems from the long-standing tradition in regional economic analysis with the export base concept, whereby the economic fortunes of states or regions are strongly dependent upon the area's ability to sell its goods or services to nonlocal or "export" markets that may be either domestic or foreign. The income accruing to a state's firms and households from external sources then circulates throughout the economy, supporting the "local or nonbasic" economic activities. Export sectors characterized by growing demands and their dependent, expanding nonbasic sectors then attract additional capital investment and labor that contribute net new additions to the stock of the state's productive physical and human capital and labor.

Although the concept of the export base is well established, the question remains: Does selling goods and services in foreign markets result in any greater economic stimulus to state economies than selling them in domestic export markets, that is, in interstate trade? A simple answer is not apparent. Most studies of state or regional foreign exports have been confined to a documentation of the employment or other contributions of exports to state economic activity (e.g., Fieleke, 1986; Florida Department of Commerce, 1989; Gillespie, 1982; Griffin, 1989; Smith, 1989), and few have sought to unravel the nature of the exporting–economic growth relationship.

There is some empirical evidence that state foreign exports are associated with higher multiplier effects than production for domestic consumption. Coughlin and Cartwright (1987b) have provided a more extensive analysis of state export-related employment estimates than those possible using the standard export employment estimates from the ASM or CM. Although the ASM and CM data capture the employment generated by the direct manufacture of exports, the related upstream production of intermediate goods and services, and the downstream trade margins and shipping to ports, these authors argue that there is an additional employment effect. They regard exports as an autonomous increase in aggregate demand which generates additional employment multiplier effects, and proceed to specify a time-series model in which state nonagricultural employment is a function of lagged employment and real industrial exports.

Coughlin and Cartwright (1987b) estimated the model for each of the fifty states in separate regression equations, focusing on the slope of the parameter relating real exports to nonagricultural employment. The model generally performed well, with R^2 values exceeding .7 for over 80 percent of the states. The parameter estimates for real exports were of the anticipated (positive) sign and significant at the .10 level or better for all but three of the states. The average short-run elasticity measuring the response of nonagricultural employment to a change in real exports was .21, indicating that a one percent increase in real exports would cause a .21 percent change in state employment. There was also evidence of substantial variation in the elasticities among states, which ranged from .089 to .348 in the short run and from .195 to .583 in the long run.

In a subsequent article, Webster et al. (1990) argued the need to carry Coughlin and Cartwright's (1987b) analysis further, to examine whether foreign exports have a higher multiplier effect than domestic exports. Such a finding would strengthen the case for state export promotion assistance. Webster et al. (1990) believe the prospects for higher foreign trade multipliers result from several factors. Because manufactured exports are typically more capital intensive than domestic market production, the more human capital-intensive export sectors are also typically associated with higher wage rates per worker. These higher wages lead to higher multiplier effects for export sectors in the initial round of spending, although there would presumably be no difference in subsequent rounds. In addition, these authors argue that the foreign export process is more complex (involving foreign language, greater documentation, currency conversion, export financing, international transportation, etc.) and could therefore involve greater state interindustry linkages than production for domestic markets.

Based on a variant of the traditional economic base multiplier, Webster et al. (1990) specify a model to compare the employment multipliers for both foreign exports and domestic exports using ASM exports by place of production for 1985 and 1986 for each of the fifty states and eighteen two-digit Standard Industrial Classification (SIC) manufacturing sectors. Two specifications were estimated in which total private state employment was regressed on lagged manufacturing foreign export employment in one equation and lagged manufacturing domestic export in the other. In cross-sectional estimations, both lagged foreign and domestic manufacturing export employment were highly significant variables and the equations accounted for most of the variation in state employment; however, the foreign export coefficient was nearly five times as large as the domestic export coefficient. When the equations were estimated for individual two-digit SIC manufacturing sectors, the foreign export coefficients were statistically significant and greater than the domestic export coefficients in ten equations. The reverse was true for only five SIC groups, most of which are traditionally regarded as strongly oriented to domestic markets (food and kindred products; petroleum and coal products; rubber and plastics; stone, clay, and glass; and primary metals).

Similarly, my own research found that industrial exporting is positively related to the growth in state export employment (Erickson, 1989). The Pearson correlation coefficient between direct foreign exports shipments growth from 1977–1986 and state manufacturing employment growth over the same period across the forty-eight contiguous states was .56 while the coefficient for total (direct plus indirect) export shipments and employment growth was .68 over the same period. Correlation coefficients substituting value added for manufacturing growth were nearly as high.

However, I went on to argue that a case could also be made wherein higher rates of state industrial growth actually lead to higher rates of state manufacturing export activity (Erickson, 1989). I noted that there is no strong evidence concerning the causal direction of the exporting–state industrial growth relationship from these correlations or the findings of Coughlin and Cartwright (1987b). Indeed, a substantial body of regional economic theory (i.e., the economic base) is premised on the notion that exports arising from local production surpluses are sold externally and thereby generate income to support local consumption. Further empirical evidence (Erickson, 1989) indicates that the change in the ratio of direct export to domestic value of shipments growth is not significantly related to state manufacturing employment growth. In other words, those states which shifted relatively more of their output to export markets over the 1977–1986 period did not experience any higher rates of industrial employment or value added growth. Thus, there is considerable doubt concerning the causal nature of the exporting–state-industrial-growth relationship.

In a forthcoming study of economic change using an expanded version of conventional shift-share analysis, Markusen et al. (1991) examined the role of international trade and productivity effects on regional job growth. The "national growth" and "industry mix" components were decomposed into four further components representing trade (exports, imports, and domestic demand) and productivity effects. These authors found that the ability to satisfy domestic demand was more important than trade or productivity in explaining positive growth differentials for the nine multistate U.S. Census regions over the years 1978 to 1986.

While the research by Markusen et al. (1991) and me (Erickson, 1989) does not refute the positive and significant relationship between exporting and state industrial growth, it raises serious questions concerning the nature of the causal chain. An alternative and highly plausible theory is that export growth in states and regions really emerges from sectors that perform well in domestic markets. This perspective on exporting is also more consistent with the "new theory of international trade," in which trade occurs among countries with similar demand structures for differentiated products (in contrast to traditional trade theory based on comparative advantage and factor endowments). In this emerging body of theory, export growth is most pronounced in sectors with a strong position in domestic markets and among those characterized by significant scale economies (Krugman, 1980; Hanink, 1988). While there are no definitive answers yet, the evidence strongly suggests that growth in a state's exports emerges from a solid competitive position in growing domestic markets. As Markusen et al. (1991) conclude, "state and local policymakers, enamored with visions of international trade, ought not to lose sight of the importance of domestic markets" (p. 19).

State Export Promotion Programs

State governments have been actively involved, directly or indirectly, in export promotion for several decades. As Posner (1984) notes, there are many ways in which states can influence the export environment for constituent firms. State governments may indirectly affect exports through their taxation and regulation policies. States may also affect exports directly through public programs to stimulate the sale of goods and services to other nations.

Export promotion programs have had a particularly strong impetus for development in those states where the economy is (was) intimately tied to the export of merchandise produced in a limited set of major industries (Archer and Maser, 1989). Export programs were also logical complements to state international activities that were actively used to attract foreign direct investment during the 1960s and 1970s. Indeed, recent research has shown that the destinations of industrial export flows from U.S. multistate regions are closely related to the international pattern of foreign direct investment among these regions of the country (Erickson and Hayward, 1991a).

Although state export promotion activities have been occurring for many years, these programs became more formalized and, in many respects, came of age during the 1980s, undoubtedly spurred on by the back-to-back recessions early in the decade. They have also experienced a substantial increase in the level of public resources devoted to their activities. Based on averages from the data reported for thirty-six states in FY 1984, aggregate state expenditures on international programs were probably around $30 million with a corresponding state average of nearly $600 thousand (NASDA, 1984). While there are no precise data regarding the share of these expenditures devoted to export promotion, it was probably little, if any, greater than a third of the total. In contrast, aggregate FY 1990 state expenditures on international programs were approximately $100 million (based on data for forty-four states), nearly $2 million per state (NASDA, 1991). This rate of increase in program expenditures is many times greater than the rate of inflation and far greater than the growth of total state spending during this period. Similarly, the average staff among the states' international programs has doubled over the 1984 to 1990 period to a current level of seventeen persons. Only five states experienced declines in their appropriations between 1988 and 1990. Currently, half of the typical state's international budget is devoted to export promotion.

The general array of state export promotion activities is identified in table 3.1 which includes the percentage of states with selected types of programs in FY 1990. These programs can be grouped into several

Table 3.1   Percentage of States with Selected Export Promotion Activities

Activity	1984	1990
Public/private partnerships	*	84
Multistate trade group	*	88
Separate international newsletter	32	64
How-to-export guide book	32	38
In-house consulting	86	100
Trade lead program	84	92
State matchmaker program	43	62
Seminars/conferences	93	100
Trade development training	43	86
Governor's international advisory committee	43	62
Export financing assistance	27	30
Foreign sales corporations	**	16
Trade shows/missions	77	100
Foreign offices	66	86
Number of states responding	44	50

Source: NASDA (1984; 1991).

*information not solicited in 1984 survey

**not available for use until passage of 1984 Tax Act

broad categories of activity including network and partnership arrangements, information dissemination, training programs for state and local officials, foreign sales promotion, and export financing.

Most states currently participate in some form of multistate trade promotion group(s). Such groups are typically organized to undertake general export promotion activities, conduct joint planning and strategy sessions, and share information on trade leads and costs of trade missions and shows. Similarly, various forms of public/private partnerships to promote local networking among actual and potential exporters seem to have gained in popularity during the past few years. Such programs often include mentoring schemes in which established export firms provide information based on operating experiences to fledgling exporters. These programs, because they utilize considerable donated time and resources of many business executives and require only a coordinating staff role, have added relatively little to the costs of state programs while simultaneously tapping an extensive wealth of exporting knowledge that exists within a state's businesses.

The export-related information services provided by states are many in number and reflect considerable similarity among the states. All states have some form of seminar or conference series on exporting, and all but three operate a trade lead service to disseminate information about opportunities in foreign markets (table 3.1). About three-fifths of the states have formal matchmaker programs that seek to identify specific buyers, agents, and distributors for state firms. Each of the states also operates an in-house consulting service that typically provides general trade information (e.g., exchange rates), limited market research studies, and referral services for insurance, shipping companies, brokers, credit matters, and legal assistance. While the number of states publishing separate international trade newsletters has grown considerably since 1984 (table 3.1), relatively few additional states have deemed it useful to publish "how-to-export" guidebooks.

It is generally acknowledged that the bulk of these informational services are directed to small- and medium-sized firms, most of whom are new to exporting. Given that many researchers believe a certain "capacity to export" in terms of the company's human and physical resources must exist before exporting can occur effectively (Hirsch, 1971), the orientation of the typical export promotion programs to predominantly small firms has raised questions concerning the prospects for goal achievement among state export promotion agencies. The orientation of export programs to small firms may also be inconsistent with the proposition that the export success of firms emerges from a position of growth and strength in domestic markets.

Trade development training has become a more important function of state export promotion agencies in recent years. This training function usually focuses on informing and sensitizing public officials in other state agencies, local governments, and partnerships or networks to the export promotion resources of state and federal agencies. There has also been some increase in the number of states that use a Governor's International Advisory Committee (table 3.1), a group that advises the governor about program initiatives, target areas and industries, and other facets of the export promotion enterprise.

Relatively few states provide export financing assistance; only fifteen states currently have funded and operational programs, a share that is little changed from earlier in the decade (table 3.1). Those with programs are more likely to provide loan guarantees than actual credit. Only California, Maryland, and Minnesota have a significant volume of loan guarantees, and only Illinois and New York have a 1990 loan volume of more than $5 million (NASDA, 1991). Several states have constitutional prohibitions barring government from becoming involved in such credit-providing arrangements, and many others apparently have not seen fit to advance credit for what may be perceived as a risky, competitive (with a state's existing private financial institutions), costly (at least in terms of an initial pool of loan funds), and unnecessary dimension to the state's array of export promotion activities.

Many of the aforementioned dimensions of state export promotion programs are predominantly "supply side" endeavors that aim to change the relative competitiveness of a state's constituent firms in export markets. However, the research noted above by Erickson and Hayward (1991b) suggests that supply-side approaches may have a limited ability to enhance the relative export efficiency of firms and industry sectors in a given state.

Export marketing and sales promotion is a major "demand-side" function of state government programs; these activities have been growing in relative importance. All of the states are involved in export trade show activities and hosting or sponsoring various trade missions (table 3.1). A few states also provide small grants to individual companies to display at trade shows when it appears appropriate for business creation and the state delegation is not attending. Continuing visibility in foreign markets to gather trade leads, base other operations, and attract foreign direct investment is now deemed critically important. By 1990, 86 percent of the states had at least one foreign office operated by their own staff or under contract with a private organization to further the state's interests (table 3.1); many states have multiple offices. Foreign offices represent a substantial cost component of state programs. Some states have found that a limited and less costly presence through a contractor is better than no visibility, while others have been forced to use contractors when state government salary maximums are too low for state employees to live in high-cost foreign locations. Finally, a few states have organized "shared foreign sales corporations" (table 3.1), a device authorized in the 1984 Tax Act that permits up to twenty-five unrelated businesses to run their foreign sales income through a kind of offshore financial operation in one of several U.S. possessions or other qualifying foreign jurisdictions that results in tax advantages for the participating firms. However, some states apparently perceive these shared foreign sales corporations to be a kind of "Banana Republic" scheme, and Minnesota and Louisiana have recently discontinued their use (NASDA, 1991).

Posner (1984) has staunchly supported the state government role in export promotion activities. He argues that the states are a very appropriate level of government through which export promotion can be achieved, and that they do not duplicate federal efforts. The federal government is too removed from the daily operating environment of most firms and must necessarily be more concerned with the larger trade issues of tariffs, quotas, and regulation. Local governments neither have the resources nor the expertise to engage effectively in export promotion. Despite these and other strong endorsements for a state role, empirically based research evaluating the effectiveness of state export promotion programs is practically nonexistent.

Coughlin and Cartwright (1987a) have provided an indication of the overall contribution of export promotion activities to state industrial exports. Using a cross-sectional generalized least squares analysis for 1980, the authors regressed the absolute volume of state industrial exports on state export promotion expenditures and several control variables. These control variables—reflecting a traditional factor endowments approach—were measures of physical capital, human capital, and labor. The authors found a statistically significant coefficient of .432 for export promotion expenditures, indicating that a $432,000 increase in state industrial exports will be generated by each $1,000 increase in state export promotion expenditures. Export promotion elasticities were calculated for each state that ranged from 0.0004 (Louisiana) to 0.529 (Alaska).

Although the results of Coughlin and Cartwright's (1987a) analysis provides positive evidence of effectiveness for proponents of a strong state role in export promotion, the results are not unambiguous. The causal structure of the model is certainly open to question. The authors' specification implies that promotion expenditures "generate" exports, but it is equally plausible that states with stronger export (and domestic) economies may be better able to fund export promotion activities. The use of factor endowments theory as the basis for control variable selection also limits the scope of elements that could account for variations in export performance. A fully specified model may eliminate the significance of the promotion variable or change its magnitude substantially. Finally, the wide range of values for export promotion elasticities for states is cause for some concern, that is, why should Louisiana and Alaska experience such widely divergent results for their export promotion expenditures (a factor of 132 times)?

State Export Promotion: Programs in Search of a Paradigm

In the absence of a solid base of program evaluation, states have largely been left to "follow the leader(s)" in terms of policy directions. The broad categorical similarities among state programs attest to the diffusion of ideas concerning what are deemed to be desirable elements of a well-rounded export promotion enterprise. Perhaps the fact that state export promotion programs have historically represented a relatively small share of total state expenditures is responsible for the paucity of evaluative studies and the ability of promotion agencies to perpetuate their existence on more impressionistic arguments before agency executives and legislators.

The evaluation of the effectiveness of state export promotion policies, like more other governmental programs, will not be an easy task. The causal structure of complex and interrelated elements in the export economy and state promotion almost defies rigorous quantitative analysis. In addition, the programs operated by the various states have their own special features and adaptations that make the development of typologies and structural analysis a difficult task. Macro analyses may lead to very spurious results and invalid conclusions about program effectiveness.

Based on their analysis of survey and secondary information on state export promotion efforts, Kudrle and Kite (1989) offer several observations concerning program evaluation. First, the general underinvestment in internal monitoring and evaluation of international programs may lead to a "backlash" when public officials and taxpayers, faced with financial crises, are offered only anecdotal evidence. Second, better monitoring and evaluation improvements could be instituted at modest costs. Third, far more attention needs to be devoted to evaluating those activities such as seminars, workshops, and counseling that represent large shares of an international agency's activities. Finally, the success of programs depends on strong leadership with well-understood objectives.

Such prescriptions, while representing useful perspectives on program management, ignore the absence of an underlying theory of export behavior of firms. Unfortunately, theoretical research is limited regarding the types of firms that have a higher probability of engaging in export trade, even though Hirsch (1971) and other scholars have argued that firm characteristics are significant determinants of variations in export activity. McConnell (1979) was able to discriminate between exporting and nonexporting firms based upon a variety of behavioral and other characteristics of the enterprises and their management. He concluded that typical exporting firms have management with a high propensity for risk-taking and an aggressive and competitive marketing strategy; exporter firms are also characterized by medium-range levels of total sales. In contrast, nonexporting firms were characterized by low-risk propensity and more conservative strategies; they were primarily small, locally based firms. Similarly, Suzman and Wortzel (1984) have suggested numerous forces that highlight differences between exporters and nonexporters. Other studies have attempted to profile the progressive stages of the "internationalization" of firms (Hayter, 1986; LeHeron, 1980; McConnell, 1982) and examine their export strategies (Namiki, 1988). Each displays the fundamental assumption that firms engaged in exporting exhibit distinctly different characteristics from those not exporting and that profiles of firms can be constructed based upon those characteristics.

There is also a paucity of hard evidence concerning the existing foreign markets in which a state's exports are sold. Such marketing information could prove extremely useful in better targeting demand-enhancing sales programs. Recent research has found that significant differences exist in the foreign destinations of industrial exports among nine multistate U.S. regions (Erickson and Hayward, 1991a); however, such market identification research has not yet been accomplished for individual states. In the absence of such information, states are prone to overlook such massive existing markets as Canada, focusing instead on those areas in which other states are currently establishing offices and missions in a typical follow-the-leader fashion.

Thus, future research on state export promotion policies must focus on two parallel tracks. The first includes basic research to uncover the underlying factors and processes that lead firms to export their products in foreign markets and the identification of those markets along with changing patterns over time. The second includes applied policy research on the effectiveness of state export promotion programs, focusing on specific program goals, monitoring of firm progress after assistance is provided, and the verification of critical causal relationships between pro-grams and outcomes. Armed with these kinds of information, state policymakers should be better able to make intelligent decisions about resource allocation and strategies in export promotion.

FOUR

GOVERNMENT EFFORTS TO PROMOTE INTERNATIONAL TRADE: STATE TRADE OFFICES IN JAPAN[1]

Ruth M. Grubel

THE U.S. relationship with Japan, which former Ambassador Mike Mansfield called "the most important bilateral relationship, bar none," is experiencing tension. Because Japan is now the world's biggest creditor and the United States is the biggest debtor, resentment has escalated over economic policies in both countries. Even with the uncertainties of the Gulf war, and a serious downturn in Japan's stock market during 1990, its economy is expected to grow by 3 percent in 1991 (Brauchli, 1991), so the Japanese market should be capable of absorbing more U.S. exports. Nevertheless, relatively few American businesses are selling to Japan, and threats of reprisal are made by politicians who perceive that Japanese trade barriers are preventing further sales in that nation.

The declining but persistent trade deficit with Japan which was $38 billion in 1990 is only one source of irritation. During the recent crisis in the Persian Gulf region, Japan's refusal to send troops to assist with the liberation of Kuwait was seen by many Americans as evidence of irresponsibility, even though Japan promised to contribute $13 billion towards war-related costs. Furthermore, high-profile purchases of well-known U.S. landmarks by Japanese investors have contributed to anxiety among some Americans.[2] In a poll of the Americans Talk Security series, 59 percent of the respondents agreed with the statement "our economic competitors like Japan pose more of a threat to our national security than our traditional military adversaries like the Soviets," and 55 percent agreed that "Japan and Western Europe's strong economies hurt U.S. national security because they threaten our own economy" (Saikowski, 1988; Morin, 1988).

Because of negative attention focused on the trade deficit with Japan, political forces mobilized in Congress to pass the Omnibus Trade Bill, and were successful in urging President Reagan to sign the legislation during his last year in office, despite his original resistance to "protectionist" policies. However, the multiple elements of this law only serve to emphasize the diffusion of trade efforts among a variety of federal agencies without a strong coordinating body which would articulate a comprehensive policy position, particularly toward Japan.

In contrast to the diverse and sometimes damaging trade efforts made at the federal level, state governments have begun cultivating ties with Japanese firms and agencies in hopes of tapping the Japanese market and investment capital. There are more U.S. state trade offices in Japan than in any other nation. Governors regularly lead state trade delegations to Japan, and they make efforts to encourage Japanese investments in their states as well.

Although trade missions and offices in Tokyo are publicized as indicators of state efforts for economic development, dealing with Japan can be a very costly enterprise. In this era of limited resources and budgetary constraints, as well as public concern over growing foreign ownership of U.S. assets, there are questions about the political and financial prudence of appropriations for offices or consultants in Japan. What kind of political support is necessary to initiate and sustain state economic relations with Japan?

This chapter will first examine the federal government's position on trade policy and the issues which have made the states the most active public sector players in promoting trade with Japan. Then the political dynamics within the states which incubate these potentially controversial international economic development efforts will be analyzed by focusing specifically on the establishment of state trade offices in Japan.

Federal Shortcomings in Alleviating the U.S. Trade Deficit with Japan

Although the yen has dramatically risen in value against the dollar since 1985 (in May 1985, $1.00 equalled 252 yen, but by early 1991, the rate was approximately 135 yen) Japan's trade surplus with the United States has persisted. The Reagan administration had maintained that a weaker dollar would automatically make American products easier to sell abroad, and Japanese imports made more expensive by the new currency values would be shunned by U.S. consumers. However, the devalued dollar did not accomplish this expected reversal in the trade deficit, and increasing pressure was placed on the President to approve the 1988 Trade Bill aimed at reducing barriers to U.S. exports. In fact, pressure was particularly evident because during the election year, the administration did not wish to be perceived as insensitive to domestic industries suffering from foreign competition.

Because of decentralization trends in Congress (propelled by the increase in numbers of subcommittees in the 1970s), individual legislators had also been approached by growing numbers of special interest groups, including those wishing protection from foreign import competition. However, these increased lobbying efforts reflected additional changes taking place in international economic relations. Destler (1986) identifies the combined effects of the globalization of the U.S. economy, its decline from hegemony in world trade, disillusionment with the free trade concept, and the rise in the dollar's value in the early 1980s as creating an environment for protectionist tendencies among significant sectors of the public and business elites. Furthermore, even with the United States Trade Representative's (USTR) office expanded under the Carter administration, trade issues were being handled by a myriad of federal agencies. For example, the active secretary of commerce (Malcolm Baldrige) in the Reagan cabinet competed against the USTR (William Brock) for leadership in trade issues. With further involvement by the departments of State, Treasury, and Agriculture, as well as others, it became more difficult for the president to exert strong leadership in foreign trade issues. Without presidential leadership, congressional self-discipline, or shared respect between the executive and legislative branches, the attainment of a free trade perspective became very difficult (Pastor, 1980).

In *Making Foreign Economic Policy* (1980), Destler recommends that a decentralized policymaking process should include a small coordinating or brokering group based in the Executive Office of the President to ensure that all positions on a foreign economic issue can be represented. Without such a coordinating staff, the divergent efforts to create trade policy often culminate in legislation such as the 1,000-page 1988 Trade Bill which attempted to respond to multiple interest group demands.

In hearings before the Subcommittees on Asian and Pacific Affairs and International Economic Policy and Trade of the House Committee on Foreign Affairs in 1984 (*United States-Japan Relations*), George Packard, dean of the Johns Hopkins School of Advanced International Studies, praised the Reagan Administration for creating a personal relationship between the president and Japan's Prime Minister Nakasone, as well as for retaining the very respected Mike Mansfield as U.S. ambassador in that country. However, Packard faulted the administration for not utilizing professional Japan specialists in policy making positions, and for setting multiple, confusing priorities in regard to Japan because of competition among at least six agencies involved with U.S.-Japan relations. In contrast to Destler's suggestion of a brokering group in the EOP, Packard recommended the creation of a "supra-cabinet level coordinator for Japan policy" to ensure that there would be better integration of priorities developed by various agencies (p. 77).

Although the specific suggestions vary somewhat, most experts on U.S.–Japan relations agree that this important ally deserves a coherent set of communications emanating from Washington, D.C. (see Destler, et al., 1976:194). However, the serious nature of the trade deficit and the resulting tension in the world economy require more than a federal Japan affairs office. In fact, contrary to popular belief, the removal of all Japanese trade barriers would not, in itself, ameliorate the trade imbalance (Bergsten and Cline, 1987:118; Lincoln, 1988:231). Instead, both Japan and the United States must participate in addressing macroeconomic conditions which threaten to amplify the already grave economic problems they share.

Efforts to deal with macroeconomic issues such as the huge U.S. budget deficit can be made only at the federal level. In fact, Tsurumi (1987) believes that a more competitive economy, which is an integral element of a healthy trade posture, cannot be achieved without federal participation in planning for research and development, worker retraining, and even funding for elementary and secondary education (p. 227). Moreover, U.S. pressure on the Japanese government to make changes in the tax laws and to implement financial deregulation should properly emanate from a well orchestrated federal endeavor (Lincoln, 1988:290). In fact, such macroeconomic issues have been addressed in the 1990 Structural Impediment Initiative talks between Japan and the United States, but whether bilateral efforts to tackle long-entrenched conditions are successful or not, there will continue to be protectionist demands made of both governments from domestic interests threatened by imports.

Although several recent U.S. administrations have attempted to avoid enacting protectionist policies by emphasizing export promotion instead (Destler, 1986:91, 92), recent federal trade legislation includes relatively few plans to assist nonfarm exporters. Particularly when dealing with Japan, many potential exporters in the United States are overwhelmed by the differences in language, customs, business practices, and legal requirements. Because of this assumed difficulty in selling foreign products in Japan, it is unlikely that Japan would be considered as a market by most small to mid-sized U.S. firms without some assistance (Fried, Trezise, and Yoshida, 1983:67). Currently, this need for export assistance is being provided, in part, by various organs of state governments.

State Entry into Foreign Trade Promotion

Several historical factors have contributed to states' involvement in foreign trade. First, the general economic slowdown which manifested itself in the mid-1970s forced business leaders and state officials to search for new markets and opportunities. The growing interdependence of the world economy suggested that foreign markets could supplement those that were waning domestically. The second catalyst for state government initiative in foreign trade was the relinquishment of that role by federal agencies. As described earlier, interagency and interbranch conflicts prevented the federal government from establishing a strong leadership in trade promotion.

Federal agencies such as the Commerce Department's Economic Development Administration and U.S. and Foreign Commercial Service, which has 47 offices in the United States and 127 offices in sixty-six other countries, certainly offer important services to businesses and even state governments (Pilcher, 1985:23). However, inadequate funding in these and other federal trade agencies has led to criticisms about the quality of service they provide (Neuse, 1982:60). As a recognition of their inadequacy, these federal agencies, members of Congress, and even presidents, have urged state governments to become more involved with trade promotion. The Department of Commerce under the Kennedy Administration encouraged state efforts in international economics, and President Carter, a former governor himself, requested that the National Governors' Association (NGA) establish a standing committee on International Trade and Foreign Relations in 1978 (Kincaid, 1984:103).

Any concerns about the constitutional propriety of state involvement in foreign trade matters were squarely addressed by the NGA and the first chair of the International Trade and Foreign Relations committee, Governor Busbee of Georgia. According to the governor, the Constitution's Commerce Clause should not be used to counteract the power of state governments to provide for their citizens' needs in health, safety, or welfare (in this case, economic welfare). The NGA went on to articulate its members' expanded roles in international trade. "States should be given full access to and, where approriate, full participation in the federal decision-making and implementation processes controlling international trade restraint and trade promotion programs when such processes significantly affect state interests" (Kline, 1983:124).

In the last twenty years, state governments have been invigorated by reforms in administrative structures, large numbers of new, more highly trained employees, and the will to confront in innovative ways, problems experienced by their constituents (Anton, 1987:729). The pursuit of economic development is such an endeavor, wherein state governments are eclipsing federal attempts to vitalize the economy. As one component of these economic development efforts, foreign trade, and particularly the establishment of foreign trade offices, has become a common activity for the states.

State Trade Offices in Japan

In order to assess current state foreign office activities, and to supplement data published by the National Association of State Development Agencies (NASDA) in 1984, 1985, 1986, and 1991, the appropriate agency in each state was contacted by telephone. Questions focused on the establishment of Japan trade offices and the cost of operating those offices.

In spite of the relative high cost of establishing and maintaining foreign offices, states are opening new operations each year. In 1977, twenty-two states had overseas offices (Kline, 1983:59), but by 1990, forty-two states had 163 offices (see table 4.1). With a total of 41, Japan has the largest number of state trade offices, almost twice as many as Taiwan, which has 22 offices, the second most numerous (NASDA, 1991:750). Some of these are full-fledged store-front offices, each representing a single state and with several full-time employees. Inevitably, such offices are very costly and may require in excess of half a million dollars per year. Other offices may simply involve the occasional services of a consultant on contract to the state, or even an honorary attache who represents the state from time to time.

Although the locations for these foreign offices vary according to markets for state products, most states have representation in both Europe and Asia. It is noteworthy that even states which originally opened offices in other Asian countries such as Taiwan and Korea, and in Hong Kong, are establishing representation in Japan as well. Table 4.1 indicates the growth in numbers of Japan trade offices even during the 1988–90 period when the strong yen has made such endeavors major ticket items in most state budgets. Although it comes as no surprise that a large, coastal state such as California spends over $600,000 on its Japan office, North Dakota, with a total annual international economic development budget of

Table 4.1   State Trade Offices, 1984, 1986, 1988, 1990

	1984	1986	1988	1990
Number of All State Trade Offices	54	69	108	163
(percent in Japan)	(31)	(35)	(35)	(25)
Number of State Japan Trade Offices	17	24	38	41
Number of States with Trade Offices	29	32	44	42
(percent with Japan office)	(59)	(75)	(86)	(93)

Source: Data gathered from 1988 telephone interviews with state international development representatives and NASDA State Export Program Database (1991, 1986).

$211,153, appropriated $91,755 (43 percent) in 1990 for its only foreign trade office in Japan (see table 4.2).

Among the state economic development officers asked about any resistance to spending for Japan trade offices, the response usually indicated that there was wide agreement that the financial returns in export contacts and reverse investment far outweighed the state expenditures for those offices. Some state economic development offices make a point of publicizing the financial benefits of the foreign operations in order to maintain budgetary support. For example, in 1981, New York's representative in Tokyo reported that his office generated $10 million in export business (Kline, 1983:61). Although such figures are somewhat unreliable because it is difficult to determine just what proportion of a particular business deal is attributable to state trade office activity, most states now compile evidence of commercial successes.

Table 4.2   Foreign Trade Offices

State	Japan Office Location	Japan Office Budget		Total Number of Offices	
		1988	1990	1988	1990
Alabama	Tokyo	$300,000	$270,000	5	3
Alaska	Tokyo	400,000	367,000	2	3
Arizona	none			1	1
Arkansas	Tokyo	150,000	NA	3	3
California	Tokyo	660,000	694,000	2	5
Colorado	Tokyo	150,000	200,000	2	3
Connecticut	Tokyo	150,000 (1986)	NA	2	2
Delaware	Tokyo	200,000	160,000	1	3
Florida	Tokyo	96,000	350,000	4	6
Georgia	Tokyo	387,000	510,000	4	5
Hawaii	Tokyo	NA	140,000	1	2
Idaho	none			1	2
Illinois	Osaka	300,000	NA		
	Tokyo	420,000	NA	6	11
Indiana	Tokyo	229,432 (1986)	NA	4	6
Iowa	Tokyo	300,000	302,000	3	3
Kansas	Tokyo	175,000	NA	2	9
Kentucky	Tokyo	355,000	NA	2	4
Louisiana	Tokyo	75,000	100,000	4	3
Maine	none			0	0
Maryland	Tokyo	140,000 (1986)	470,000	2	6
Massachusetts	Tokyo	NA	NA	0	1
Michigan	Tokyo	350,000	691,000	3	5
Minnesota	Osaka	NA	35,000		
	Tokyo	none	37,000	2	8
Mississippi	Tokyo	none	25,000	2	3

(Continued next page)

Table 4.2   (Continued)

State	Japan Office Location	Japan Office Budget 1988	Japan Office Budget 1990	Total Number of Offices 1988	Total Number of Offices 1990
Missouri	Tokyo	NA	NA	3	4
Montana	Tokyo	434,000	243,000	2	2
Nebraska	Tokyo (to 1983)			0	0
Nevada	Tokyo	NA	50,000	1	3
New Hampshire	none			0	0
New Jersey	Tokyo	NA	50,000	2	1
New Mexico	none			0	0
New York	Tokyo	200,000 (1986)	NA	6	5
North Carolina	Tokyo	NA	NA	4	4
North Dakota	Tokyo	50,000	91,755	1	1
Ohio	Tokyo	200,000 (1986)	411,110	3	5
Oklahoma	Tokyo	NA	NA	5	4
Oregon	Tokyo	NA	1,200,000	3	3
Pennsylvania	Tokyo	157,000	NA	3	3
Rhode Island	none			2	3
South Carolina	Tokyo	200,000	NA	2	3
South Dakota	none			0	0
Tennessee	none			0	0
Texas	Tokyo	none	NA	1	6
Utah	Tokyo	200,000	168,000	3	4
Vermont	Tokyo	50,000	none	2	0
Virginia	Tokyo	133,000 (1986)	350,000	2	2
Washington	Tokyo	NA	318,000	1	2
West Virginia	Nagoya	none	250,000	0	1
Wisconsin	Tokyo	400,000	637,100	3	4
Wyoming	none			1	1

Source: Data gathered from 1988 telephone interviews with state international development representatives and NASDA State Export Program Database (1991, 1986).

In some cases, however, even marketing breakthroughs were not enough to support a state office in Japan. For example, in the late 1970s both California and Nebraska had trade offices in Tokyo. Later, Governor Brown's administration in California placed domestic issues ahead of foreign trade, so all overseas offices were closed. A Tokyo office was then reopened in 1986 under a new administration. For Nebraska, the farm crisis and state financial problems forced the Tokyo office to be regarded as an extravagance, so it was closed in 1983. Although Nebraska has not established a new office, the economic development department maintains employees with expertise in Japanese affairs who described in an interview the hope that an office will be reopened there in the early 1990s. More recently, recessionary trends are causing severe fiscal crises in many states, and the necessity of reducing government budgets may lead to the elimination of trade offices. The current economic downturn is generating careful reappraisals of trade offices. For example, Vermont closed its new Japan office in 1989, and although Wisconsin authorities are promising not to close any trade offices, cost-cutting measures enacted in response to reduced state revenues may necessitate staff changes in these offices (Norman, 1991).

In addition to the promotion of financial benefits to state businesses emphasized by development department officials, political support for Japan trade office funding can come from nonbusiness associations as well. Many states and cities have established sister state/city relationships with counterparts in Japan. Although primarily maintained for cultural and educational purposes, these ties have developed business facets as well. In 1959 the Isewan Typhoon caused severe damage in some regions of Japan. When a group of Iowa farmers heard about entire swine herds having been wiped out by the storm, they responded by donating some of their own pigs to the farmers of Yamanashi prefecture. This gesture precipitated the first Japan–U.S. sister state relationship, which continues today. Though the Iowa trade office established in 1986 is not located in Yamanashi prefecture, the longstanding ties of friendship with Japan were instrumental in generating support for the $300,000 office expenditure.

Perhaps because of Japan's reputation as a wealthy country, many of the state trade offices emphasize reverse investment, particularly by companies which move their operations to the United States. There are political risks in appearing to be selling out to foreign owners, but Japanese companies and organizations have been working hard in recent years, through lobbying and philanthropy, to improve their image. Although these efforts have succeeded in reversing unitary taxes in twelve states ("Japan's Clout," 1988), many states still maintain some forms of "buy American" restrictions which discriminate against foreign products in state purchases (Kline, 1984:3). Nevertheless, economically depressed communities such as Norman, Oklahoma, appear to support the Japanese investments which have brought jobs, even though there are questions about the origins of components being assembled in the plants ("Japan's Clout," 1988:74–75).

Some objections have also been made to large financial incentives being offered by states to attract Japanese firms such as highly publicized automobile factories. Even when such incentives are used to compete for domestic businesses, states rarely recoup their costs, and the public is ill served (Grady, 1987). However, a Nebraska economic development official mentioned that in contrast to American firms which relocate more freely according to political and financial incentives offered by different states, Japanese companies do thorough research on potential locations for their operations, and thus are more committed for the long term once they make a decision. As a result, Japanese companies are less likely to be swayed by financial incentives which can diminish the value of the business to the state.

When Japanese firms are given government incentives to locate in a particular city, the companies have sometimes taken action to reduce the cost to the public. In 1985 Mazda built a plant in Flat Rock, Michigan, where the company received a 100 percent tax abatement for twelve years. However, when sewer and street repairs necessary for the operation became a hardship for the city's budget, public support waned until Mazda promised to donate $100,000 per year during the time of the tax abatement, and even to provide $1 million for the sewer project ("Japan's Clout," 1988:74).

Even when there is not as much financial incentive competition among state offices attempting to attract Japanese investment, efforts to combine the operations of several states into one office in Japan have not been successful. Regional or multistate trade offices have been recommended by some analysts as providing significant savings over single-state offices (Archer and Maser, 1989:238; Neuse, 1982:60). However, efforts to implement such cooperative ventures have not uniformly succeeded because the competition among the states represented in these offices prevented their smooth operation.

Some states prefer to dictate the administrative aspects of their trade offices, while others hire consultants who are responsible for the day-to-day operations of their work. Depending upon the goals of particular state offices, the expertise of the personnel can vary considerably. For example, retired Japanese businessmen make up a growing segment of state trade representatives. Not only do these men (they are usually men) have established contacts in the Japanese business world, they are completely familiar with the dynamics of doing business in that country. Often, these former businessmen will have spent time in the United States during their careers, and preferably would have had experience in the states they are representing.

As the number of U.S. citizens who are acquiring experience in Japanese affairs increases, some states prefer to rely on "home-grown" trade representatives who are more knowledgeable about conditions in their own state. Still other states choose trade officers who have expertise in disciplines and industries of greatest interest to the state.

If a state's economy has strong links to Japan, operations of the trade office may be expanded. As shown in table 4.2, Illinois has two Japan trade offices. Although an office in Osaka had been maintained since 1983, the location of many new Japanese companies in Illinois warranted the state's additional representation in the Tokyo market, so a second office was opened there in 1987, even at the high cost of another $420,000.

Table 4.2 also indicates that all but three of the state trade offices are located in Tokyo. In Minnesota's case, the person originally hired to represent the state had ties to Osaka businesses, but another office was open later in Tokyo as well. Real estate and office costs in the Osaka/Kansai area are rapidly rising to approach the world's highest rates in Tokyo, so funding an office in either city is extremely expensive. Because Japan is a geographically small country, and transportation services are excellent, establishing a trade office in a less expensive Japanese city would presumably provide just as much accessibility to business contacts, but at considerable savings. West Virginia is the only state with an office in Nagoya, a major city between Tokyo and Osaka. The fact that most state Japan offices are in Tokyo, however, indicates that there are valuable advantages to an address in that city. In Japan, appearances are of prime importance, and in business, one of the indications of success and power is an office in Tokyo. Therefore, not only does having an office in Tokyo allow a state representative to be within one hour of most of Japan's major company headquarters, but also the prestige of having a Tokyo office may confer certain perception advantages for the state itself.

A state's prestige may not only assist in attracting Japanese investment but also benefit the marketing of state products as well. Because Japanese consumers find appeal in high-quality prestige products, the state trade offices can guide prospective U.S. exporters to develop appropriate product lines and promotional tactics. Naturally, the few personnel in each state office cannot provide such a broad range of marketing services for each client, but they can be effective in referring exporters to a variety of service providers. In addition to a growing number of private sector trade consultants with expertise in the Japanese market, other organizations such as the Japan External Trade Organization (JETRO), which is an arm of Japan's Ministry of International Trade and Industry (MITI), has offices in seven U.S. cities and provides assistance to businesses as well as to state economic development agencies interested in dealing with Japan.

Although the trade offices in Japan and other services of state government are increasingly able to facilitate business dealings with the Japanese, there is some question about the role of state officials in promoting foreign markets to businesses which have never considered exporting. Most development department officers polled for this study insisted that no funds are earmarked specifically for recruiting new exporters, and that providing services for self-identified exporters is their mandate. However, by publicizing their foreign offices and trade related services, as well as by acquiring broad media coverage for governors' trade missions, the states may be acting increasingly to internationalize their economies.

Discussion and Conclusions

In this brief examination of the state trade offices and their role in dealing with U.S.–Japan economic relations, it is evident that states are not only taking initiatives in economic development where the federal government has had limited participation, they are truly becoming international actors in their own rights. However, because of rising U.S. protectionism and provincialism, as well as ambivalence about Japan among many in the public, the rationale for spending significant proportions of overextended state budgets on trade offices, particularly in Japan, is increasingly questioned.

Anton (1987) argues that there are four patterns from the old politics of American federalism which have allowed innovative state programs to flourish without the backing of new political movements or overwhelming popular support. These patterns are responsiveness, elitism, pluralism, and experimentation. The trend to internationalize state economies, and more specifically, to establish trade offices in Japan, can be understood politically by using Anton's patterns.

First, state governments become involved in economic development schemes *in response* to economic problems. For many state leaders, international markets and investors were logical options to pursue growth when the domestic economy was stagnant. More recently, as the trade deficit expanded and Japan's per capita GNP at current exchange rates exceeded that of the United States, state governors and economic development departments acted to exploit opportunities in Japan.

Second, most of the decision making regarding international trade and Japan offices is done by relatively few people. Because the public as a whole tends to be more isolationist than elites, the initiatives for globalizing state economies had to come from state elites, particularly governors. Although there are no efforts to keep information on state international development away from the public, support from constituents is cultivated by emphasizing the material benefits of world trade to the state.

Anton's third pattern is called pluralist in that innovative state programs "are designed to serve well-established and influential interests" (p. 731). Export assistance efforts and reverse investments serve businesses in all regions of the states. However, because these pluralist programs usually cater to established business interests, there is an assumption that benefits will only eventually accrue to workers for whom more jobs and opportunities will be created. The person on the street has little evidence that a state Japan trade office puts money directly in his or her pocket.

Finally, state international development activities are definitely experimental. Because international trade offices, particularly in Japan, are a relatively new phenomenon, there is little evidence to indicate which types of activities are most successful. Will the Japanese businesses actually exploit state incentives without contributing significantly to the communities and state economies? Is the Japanese market so difficult to penetrate that not even expensive Tokyo offices will produce long-term results? Will latent provincialism erupt in a movement to close trade offices and restrict imports? Only after further experience in operating state trade offices will we learn the answers to these questions.

In order to evaluate existing state trade offices and to consider various alternatives in expediting trade with Japan, the following issues should be considered:

1. Are state trade officials duplicating services offered by private-sector agents?
2. Is there adequate oversight of trade office activities to ensure effective use of state resources and to prevent conflicts of interest among state-employed consultants?
3. Are program evaluation techniques able to discern the financial impact of Japan trade offices?
4. Is political support for a trade office broad enough to warrant planning beyond the current administration?
5. Can a trade office in Japan be effectively substituted either by a single Asian office in another country or by managing business with Japan through state support of trade shows and trade missions?
6. If a state presence in Japan is mandated, what are the comparative benefits of an honorary attache, a representative with a contract from the state, full-time staff in a state facility, or perhaps an operation shared with one or more other states?

Because every state has a different environment of economic, social, and political factors, the goals for international economic development vary significantly as well. Consideration of the questions listed above should clarify the unique conditions which are present in each state.

Notes

1. This study was funded, in part, by a Wisconsin State Research Grant. It is an updated version of a paper presented at the 1988 Annual Meeting of the American Political Science Association, Washington, D.C.
2. Although Japanese investments in U.S. capital have attracted recent media attention, in September 1987, Europeans held $745 billion in U.S. assets, while Japanese owned a total of $182 billion (Burgess, 1988, p. 7).

FIVE

PROMOTING EXPORTS FOR STATE ECONOMIC DEVELOPMENT: AN EMPIRICAL NOTE

Stephen H. Archer and Steven M. Maser

SINCE AT least the 1930s, state governments have been interested in expanding jobs and taxable income by using economic development policies to make themselves more attractive places to do business—often in competition with other states for jobs and incomes. More recently states have turned their efforts abroad, first to attract foreign investment, but more recently to promote exports from their private sectors to foreign nations (Archer and Maser, 1989). States vary not only in exports and exports per capita, but also in government support for export promotion.

A sparse literature on state export promotion looks at why some states promote their exports more aggressively, at least in a state budgetary sense. We summarize these sometimes conflicting economic and political arguments. Next we examine the limited secondary source data available in an attempt to discriminate, at least in part, valid from invalid arguments.

Propositions in the Literature

State business incentives in general and international trade activities in particular have attracted the attention of students of economic development. Amidst an ongoing debate about the productivity of the war of incentives, where states compete to attract jobs, there is doubt about the efficacy of any of these programs (O'Grady, 1987; Peretz, 1985). However, efforts to create jobs by expanding exports from states' indigenous firms have not received much attention. That is hardly surprising because quantitative information is problematic and the history of export promotion efforts is short. The literature offers several propositions but little in the way of systematic evaluation. None are particularly well rooted in political or economic theory and we shall not attempt to accomplish that here. We want simply to assess the empirical validity of the claims that others are making.

First, economic hardship or fear of it are frequently cited as explaining or justifying state government policies that encourage firms to export. The greater the unemployment in the state, the greater the state's export promotion effort (Kline, 1982), as measured in terms of budgets. As a corollary, the more concentrated the state's economy (that is, the less diversified industrially), the greater the reason for promoting exports from the less significant parts of the state's economy. The idea is to stabilize the impact of the business cycle (Pilcher and Proffer, 1985). In other words, the more concentrated the industry of the state, the more susceptible it is to the roller coaster of economic forces. For example, Boeing's decline in the 1960s led to Washington State's effort to diversify; recession in the oil patch motivated Louisiana similarly.

Conversely, some states increased their efforts, presumably to promote the exports of major state industries subject to increasing international competition. States heavily dependent on agriculture suffered dramatically as the rise in the dollar reduced that industry's export capability. The greater the importance of agriculture in the state, the greater were the arguments for export promotion by the state in the early 1980s (Pilcher and Proffer, 1985). In general, state effort increases with the increase in foreign competition and technological change; these factors can devastate a state economy (Guisinger, 1985).

Second, geographic location, that is, proximity to foreign countries or oceans (a sort of "around the edges" theory), is likely to lead to greater export promotion efforts (Kline, 1982). The level of port activity, for example, might suggest a heightened consciousness about the opportunity for exporting (Egan & Bendick, 1985), as would a state's dependence of foreign trade.

Third, if a state is already doing well in exports, one might expect to see such measures of economic well-being negatively related to state export budgets. If, for example, the value of exports makes up a relatively large proportion of all production, or the ratio of export employment to total employment is high, we might expect to see relatively small state budgets. If so, then a recent history of rising exports will induce cutbacks in state export development budgets.

Fourth, it is usually argued that large firms do not need the assistance of the state in promoting their exports; they are perfectly capable of doing it themselves. Small and medium-sized firms are less able to overcome the information costs, including market information costs, the costs of getting into the market. Therefore, the greater the proportion of small businesses in the state, the greater may be the expected payoff from the state promoting exports.

The greatest potential to increase the *number* of firms exporting is with firms having fewer than one hundred employees. The percent of small businesses, as measured by employment, varied from 98.3 percent of establishments with less than one hundred employees in South Carolina to 43.19 percent in Michigan. But, ironically, the greatest potential to increase the *total value* of exports lies in getting large firms not now exporting to export (Egan and Bendick, 1985). One study estimated that 80 percent of the value of exports was done by 1 percent of the firms. Only 10 percent of small businesses export (Czinkota, 1982; Pilcher and Proffer, 1985).

Finally, politics can intrude on decisions about both the level and type of economic development activity. It has been suggested that effective export promotion by the state requires cooperation and coordination by the executive and legislative branches of state government. Consequently, control of both by one political party may be facilitative (Pilcher and Proffer, 1985).

In summary, economic hardship or fear of it may be a factor in increasing state development attention to export promotion. Among these hardship factors were unemployment and lack of diversity of the economy, including the dominance of agriculture. Others suggested as contributing factors were export trade consciousness, the importance of small businesses, and single-party political control over the legislative and executive branches. Success in exports is expected to lead to a negative relationship with state export promotion budgets.

Examining the Propositions

To examine whether state budgets for export promotion respond to these factors, the authors collected data from secondary sources and tested the relationships posited above. The state budget data for export promotion shown in table 5.1 was available for all fifty states in 1980 (Kline, 1982) and for thirty-five states in 1984 (Price Waterhouse, 1986).[1] Relative, or per capita, emphasis on export promotion by states was obtained by dividing the total budget by the state population for the appropriate year (U.S. Bureau of Census, 1987); however, only the 1983 population is shown at the end of table 5.1.

These per capita export promotion budgets served as dependent variables, one for 1980 and one for 1984.[2] As one might expect, some of the largest states by population, such as New York, have very large budgets but, given their populations, tend to expend small amounts on a per capita basis. This suggests that some of the export promotion expenditures are invariant with population. For example, an overseas office may be a relatively small expenditure for large states on a per capita basis and a very significant expenditure for small states.[3]

Based on the suggestions in the literature and constrained by the availability of data or suitable proxies, the independent variables used for the 1980 tests were:

1. The 1980 unemployment rate for the state (U.S. Bureau of Census, 1986).
2. The ratio of agriculture exports to manufactured exports in 1982 (Price Waterhouse, 1986).
3. The percent of business establishments represented by small business (fewer than 100 employees) in 1981[4] (U.S. Small Business Administration, 1983).
4. The percent of the value of state production for export to total production for 1981 (National Governors' Association, 1985; Price Waterhouse, 1986).
5. The percent increase in state exports from 1977 to 1981 (National Governors' Association, 1985).
6. The 1982 total export tonnage of the ports of the state (U.S. Bureau of Census, 1984b).

Table 5.2 shows the results for the 1980 test using observations on forty-nine states.[5] Simple correlation coefficients between the dependent and independent variables are provided in the final column of the table. The state budget per capita showed a positive relationship to the dominance of the agricultural export industry in the state as measured by variable 2 and to the port activity variable, variable 6. As expected, there was a negative relationship with variable 5, the increase in exports of the state from 1977 to 1981. The variables without significant contribution (variables 1, 3, and 4) were deleted for the final multiple regression results reported in table 5.2.

The multiple regression produced the values for the slopes of the relationships and require some interpretation. For each 10 percent increase in the importance of agricultural exports to manufactured exports, the per capita export promotion budget increased 0.192 cents; for example if agriculture was equal to (i.e., 100 percent of) manufactured exports in 1982, then state export promotion budgets would be expected to be 1.92 cents higher for each person in the state population. For every 10 percent increase in exports from 1977 to 1981, the 1980 state export promotion budget lowered .413 cents per capita. And for every million tons of exports going through state ports (if they had one or more) in 1982, the 1980 state export budget per capita would be expected to

Table 5.1   State Export Promotion Budgets

State	1980 Budget (thousands)	Rank	1980 Budget[a] Per Capita (thousands)	Rank	1983 Population (thousands)	1984 Budget (thousands)	Rank	1984 Budget[b] Per Capita (thousands)	Rank
1 Alabama	$ 274	19	$0.0703	22	3933	$250	14	$0.0636	14
2 Alaska	372	13	0.9266	1	459			NA	
3 Arizona	107	32	0.0394	35	2949	140	21	0.0475	20
4 Arkansas	175	27	0.0766	20	2315	200	16	0.0864	10
5 California	234	23	0.0099	46	25024	368	10	0.0147	30
6 Colorado	120	30	0.0416	34	3106	150	19	0.0483	19
7 Connecticut	75	37	0.0241	39	3126	140	22	0.0448	22
8 Delaware	30	43	0.0505	27	601			NA	
9 Florida	458	11	0.0470	30	10657	520*	8	0.0488	18
10 Georgia	310	17	0.0568	24	5662	905*	4	0.1598	3
11 Hawaii	107	31	0.1111	14	964	200*	17	0.0275	2
12 Idaho	47	40	0.0503	28	982	17	34	0.0173	29
13 Illinois	1527	2	0.1336	12	11456	600	6	0.0524	17
14 Indiana	752	6	0.1370	11	5467	476	9	0.0871	9
15 Iowa	240	22	0.0825	16	2903	259	13	0.0892	8
16 Kansas	70	38	0.0296	38	2399	21	32	0.0088	33
17 Kentucky	577	10	0.1576	7	3679	42	31	0.0114	32
18 Louisiana	25	44	0.0059	49	4410			NA	
19 Maine	91	35	0.0807	18	1136			NA	
20 Maryland	1287	4	0.3053	3	4869			0.2465	
21 Massachusetts	45	41	0.0078	47	5752	75	28	0.0130	31
22 Michigan	682	9	0.0736	21	2658	844	5	0.0933	7
23 Minnesota	188	26	0.0461	31	4143			NA	
24 Mississippi	150	28	0.0595	23	2560			NA	

25 Missouri	729	8	0.1483	9	4946	580*	7	0.1173	5
26 Montana	278	18	0.3528	2	811	68*	29	0.0838	11
27 N. Carolina	503	12	0.0856	15	5971	143	20	0.0239	27
28 Nebraska	196	24	0.1247	13	1584	92	26	0.0581	15
29 Nevada	5	49	0.0063	48	885			NA	
30 New Hampshire	20	45	0.0217	41	954	0.7	35	0.0007	35
31 New Jersey	315	16	0.0428	32	7445	318	12	0.0427	23
32 New Mexico	70	39	0.0537	25	1384			NA	
33 New York	845	5	0.0481	29	17658	1000	3	0.0566	16
34 North Dakota	100	34	0.1531	8	670	20	33	0.0299	25
35 Ohio	1833	1	0.1697	6	10725	1330	1	0.1240	4
36 Oklahoma	248	21	0.0819	17	3277	350	11	0.1068	6
37 Oregon	362	14	0.1374	10	2658	1060	2	0.3988	1
38 Pennsylvania	263	20	0.0222	40	11879			NA	
39 Rhode Island	11	47	0.0119	45	951	65	30	0.0638	12
40 S. Carolina	100	33	0.0320	36	3193	94	25	0.0294	26
41 South Dakota	139	29	0.2614	5	692			NA	
42 Tennessee	194	25	0.0422	33	4667	86	27	0.0184	28
43 Texas	740	7	0.0520	26	15670	123	23	0.0078	34
44 Utah	0	50	0	50	1589	100	24	0.0680	13
45 Vermont	7	48	0.0134	44	525			NA	
46 Virginia	1487	3	0.2781	4	5396	180	18	0.0334	24
47 West Virginia	36	42	0.0183	42	1962			NA	
48 Washington	333	15	0.0806	19	4247			NA	
49 Wisconsin	82	36	0.0175	43	4746	214	15	0.0451	21
50 Wyoming	15	46	0.0319	37	512			NA	

Note: Budgets not allocated between state export promotion and promoting foreign investment in the state.

a. Per capita data computed using 1980 state population figure.

b. Per capita data computed using 1983 state population figure.

Table 5.2   State Export Promotion Explanatory Variables, 1980

Variable	B (slope value)	T Value	Prob. B=0	Simple r
2. Agricultural Dominance	+.192	3.378	.0015	+.40
5. Increase in Exports	−.413	−2.164	.0358	−.27
6. Port Export (Tons)	+.127	1.994	.0522	+.15

be higher by .127 cents. As a rough indicator of importance, we used a 95 percent statistical significance level. Only variables 2 and 5 are significant, but variable 6 is so close to the 95 percent threshold that we felt it was worth reporting. The multiple correlation coefficient was .53, whose square is .29; an adjusted r-square value was .24 and therefore the percentage of the variability of state export promotion budgets explained by variables 2, 5, and 6 was 24 percent.

One might expect that the big agricultural states felt the need to promote exports because of the vulnerability of their economies. As agricultural export promotion policies are frequently implemented by state agricultural departments and not state economic development departments, this relationship may exist out of a need to help agricultural economies by promoting agricultural exports. However, it could reflect a perceived need to promote a manufacturing (not agriculture) jobs through export promotion in order to diversify their economic bases.

The positive though not quite significant relationship with port export tonnage might support some sort of "around the edges" theory, the budget reflecting the consciousness of the international sector; thirty states of the fifty had port export tonnage. An increase in exports from 1977 to 1981 may have led those states to allocate resources to more pressing needs, hence the negative association. None of the other variables showed any significant relationship in 1980. Diversity of industry was not tested in 1980 due to the absence of data.

Lettered instead of numbered to distinguish them from the 1980 variables, the independent variables used for the 1984 test were:

A. The 1984 unemployment rate for each state.
B. The ratio of agriculture exports to manufacturing exports in 1982.
C. The percent of business establishments represented by small business in 1982.
D. A variable representing the control (or lack of) of the legislative branches of state government by a single political party in 1983 (Council of State Governments, 1983).
E. The percent of the value of production (manufactures) for export to total production (manufactured product) for 1981.

F. The percent increase in exports from 1977 to 1981.
G. The 1982 export tonnage of the port in the state.
H. The concentration (e.g., lack of diversity) of manufacturing industry in 1984.[6]

The 1984 dependent variable was state export promotion budget per capita; budget data was available for thirty-five states, but thirty-four were used in the test.[7] Table 5.3 shows the 1984 test results. The state budgets showed a positive relationship to the concentration of industry variable, variable H, and to the control of the state government by a single political party in 1984, variable D. There was a negative relationship with state export production value as a percent of total value of state production for 1981, variable E. Variables without significant explanatory value were deleted for the final multiple regression.

The multiple regression produced the values for the slopes of the relationships with the independent variables; again, some interpretation is required. With the state government in the hands of a single political party, the state budget for export promotion ran 3.5 cents higher per capita than for those where party control was divided. The concentration variable was measured by a concentration coefficient named gini, its value varying from an upper limit of 1.0 if all employment was engaged in one industry, to a value of about .05 if employment was evenly spread among twenty manufacturing industries; Hawaii was the most concentrated with a value of .7432 and Nevada was the most diversified with a value of .3194. An increase of .10 or from, say, .40 to .50 meant an increase in the average state per capita export promotion budget of 2.45 cents per capita. An increase of one in the export production percentage of the total production meant a decrease of one cent or $.01 in the per capita export promotion budget. The multiple correlation coefficient for the three significant variables was .59 and the percent of variation in state export promotion budget explained in 1984 by these three variables (D, E, and H) was 35 percent; but the adjusted coefficient of determination was .28. The unavailability of data limited the type of tests that could be made. We recognize that lagged relationships are possible here, but again lack of data limited pursuit.

Table 5.3 State Export Promotion Explanatory Variables, 1984

Variable	B (slope value)	T Value	Prob. B=0	Simple r
D. Government Control	.0350	2.087	.0455	+ .23
E. 1981 Export Production to Total	− .0100	− 2.741	.0102	− .41
H. Industry Concentration	+ .0245	2.290	.0293	+ .30

Different variables were significant in 1984 from those of the 1980 tests. However, the unemployment and small business factors were not significant in either of the two test years. Two of the three significant 1984 variables (industry concentration and government control) were not included in the 1980 test due to lack of data. And although some variables were significant in only one of the test years, certainly no conflicts were experienced. Recall that we reported the 1980 port variable even though it was not quite significant. It is not inconceivable that something as dynamic as state export promotion budgets could be influenced by factors that come in and move out of regression importance over time depending on other unknown conditions. Consequently we believe that the four significant variables (industry concentration, agricultural importance, government control and the importance of exports in the state) over the two years together can be considered as contributing influences, although we do not hesitate to admit that other variables may exist, including more fundamental ones from which our test variables may be derived.

Implications

As for the propositions offered by others to explain the pattern of budgetary support for state export promotion policies, our tests provide some interesting observations. First, although support is frequently requested to assist small business or small and medium-sized business, we find no relationship between the size of the budgets on a per capita basis and the proportion of small businesses to total businesses in the state. Reality apparently does not confirm the rhetoric behind the policy. Perhaps small businesses are not organized to be effective politically in translating requests for support into budget dollars. Indeed, the difficulty in getting small businesses (operating as they do in as large a market as the United States) to think about international markets has traditionally been a source of frustration for economic development officials.

Second, economic hardship as measured by the unemployment rate registered no significant relationship to the size of state export budgets per person in either test year. Likely, cyclical unemployment is regarded as too transitory to be a major factor in export promotion decisions, especially decisions for costly programs that require a considerable period of time to bear fruit. This coincides with O'Grady's (1987) analysis of state business incentives in general. Of course, the national unemployment rate was about the same in both our test years even though a severe recession intervened; lag effects, of course, could be involved in this highly fluctuating variable.

Still, the fear of economic hardship could have played an important role in determining these budgets. In 1980, the dominance of agricultural exports to manufactured exports was associated with budgetary support, and in 1984, the concentration of employment (i.e., lack of diversity) in certain industries showed a significant relationship. Certainly such concentration is not transitory and begs a long term solution to alleviate cyclical vulnerability in employment, income and state revenues. Here export promotion can not only help a state whose major industries are depressed, but may also contribute to greater industry diversification.

Third, if a state had a history of doing relatively well in the export area, it devoted less resources on a per capita basis to export promotion. In 1980, the percentage icrease in exports (by dollar value) from 1977 to 1981 showed a *negative* relationship to the dependent variable. This negative relationship also existed for the percentage of production for export to the total production of the state in 1984.

Fourth, the "around the edges" or "international trade consciousness" notion found slight support, because the port export tonnage data for the thirty states that had a port exhibited a weak and not significant relationship for the 1980 test. State officials, desirous of increasing export promotion activities, may have to precede this by raising the consciousness of budget-makers as well as the public about foreign opportunities. Finally, the state government control thesis had support in the 1984 test. Perhaps less bickering, albeit crudely measured, means larger budgets.

If the present is any guide to the future, then state export promotion policies will not necessarily take root and prosper in economic climates characterized by small businesses and current aggregate high unemployment. Promotion efforts are much more likely to find support in those states in which single or few industries—especially agriculture—dominate. To develop such policies, it helps if the opportunities are more readily observable, or made more observable, and a constituency of active participants, such as ports, can promote them. Universities can also play a role. Budgetary efforts are more likely to be successful with a political consensus in government, perhaps mitigating the intrastate disputes over allocating resources that characterize policy-making in local economic development. Of course, when a state's economy is heavily engaged in exporting, an aggressive policy of promoting exports for state economic development may be difficult to sustain.

Notes

1. Such economics would seem to lend support for interstate cooperation, especially among less populated states (Peretz, 1985).
2. Sources: Kline (1982), pp. 57-58; Price Waterhouse (1986), p. III-4; U.S. Bureau of the Census (1987), table 3, p. 22. Information about state budget support is contaminated by different reporting methods.

3. Although we expected to explain some of the variation in per capita export promotion budgets, it was also possible that we might be able to account for some of the change (or growth) in the relative budgets between 1980 and 1984. However, the *ratio* of 1984 to the 1980 per capita export budget as a dependent variable did not produce significant results.

4. Testing a relationship between, say, the proportion of small business in 1981 with state export promotion budget in1980 is not particularly problematic, because a big business state cannot change to a small business state in two years and therefore 1981 data should be as good as 1980 data.

5. Alaska in 1980 was such an outlier that it was discarded so as to not distort overall relationships.

6. The gini coefficient of variability of industry employment data (U.S. Bureau of Census, 1984a, table 2) was calculated to represent the concentration variable.

7. Oregon in 1984 was such an outlier that it was discarded so as to not distort the overall relationships, leaving thirty-four states in this test.

SIX

A STRATEGIC APPROACH TO STATE ECONOMIC DEVELOPMENT POLICY: THE COLORADO EXPERIENCE

Scott A. Woodard

SINCE THE 1986 gubernatorial election, economic development has been the watchword in Colorado. The major priorities of the state's top policy- and decision-makers have centered on how to position Colorado competitively both nationally and internationally. Many of their efforts have been successful; in other efforts, they have come up short. However, as never before, Coloradans are aware of their state's economy and the factors that shape it. This awareness has been driven, in large part, by the economic recession Colorado experienced between 1983 and 1988. Downturns in such mainstay industries as construction, manufacturing, and energy created a turning point for state decision-makers regarding their approach to Colorado's economic development.

As a candidate for governor, Roy Romer made economic development the cornerstone of his campaign. Once elected, Romer and his advisors created an action-oriented agenda to improve the economic development opportunities for Colorado. Immediately after his election, and prior to his inauguration, Romer began developing a strategic plan to set the direction for the state's economic development policy. Romer's process became the first in a series of seemingly competitive strategic plans, status reports, and "blueprints." Over the next two years, ten such documents were published by the Romer administration, the legislature, and the private sector. The plethora of strategic plans tended to politicize, rather than focus, economic development in Colorado.

This chapter provides a case study of one state's approach to economic development policy. It examines the development of such a policy within a political context and notes the pitfalls to avoid and the elements that are essential to success.

The Context of Economic Development in Colorado

Prior to Roy Romer's election as governor in 1986, economic development responsibilities were housed in the Department of Local Affairs with minimal staff and resources. While economic development implied the recruitment of businesses to the state, Colorado state government rarely took a proactive role in economic development leaving the initiative to local governments. Overall, Colorado's approach to economic development was fairly low key. Coloradans tended to rely on the state's reputation for scenic mountains and a relatively low tax base to attract industry.

Romer made the state's economy and its approach to economic development the cornerstone of his campaign for governor. He argued for a more aggressive approach to economic development: a stronger role for state government—especially the governor—and a partnership with the private sector to attract more firms to Colorado. His campaign significantly "raised the consciousness" of Coloradans regarding the state's economy and the investments required to help turn it around. To a large extent, Romer deserves credit for this increased awareness, for framing the issues for the state's economic improvement, and for broadening the base of participation in forming an economic development policy for Colorado. However, his approach, instead of focusing the state's economic development efforts, may well have politicized economic development.

From the outset, Romer's staff equated economic development primarily with marketing and recruitment. The perception among his economic development staff was that Colorado had been sending negative messages to firms interested in locating business operations in the state. Moreover, the current state of the economy necessitated a strong marketing initiative to lure those companies. Education and job training, infrastructure improvements, and small business assistance were often mentioned in the economic development rhetoric; but Colorado was just emerging from a severe recession and appropriate funds were not available. It should be noted that during Romer's first term (1987–1991) higher education and job training programs received substantial budget increases. However, much of the job training funds were used as incentives to attract new firms to the state.

Governor Romer also lobbied hard with Denver area voters to convince them to approve construction for a new international airport. The new airport was viewed as vital to the long-term economic viability of the state. His efforts on behalf of the proposed airport were critical to its acceptance by the voters.

For the most part, however, the major thrust of the Romer administration's economic development was to position Colorado as an attractive place for businesses to relocate. To this end, marketing campaigns extolled the low rents of Denver's overbuilt office market and the relatively high education levels of Coloradans.

Romer was as aggressive a campaigner for Colorado as he was for governor. He led marketing and business recruitment trips to Europe and Asia, as well as a number of domestic trips, to spread the word that Colorado was "open for business." Romer attempted to make the economic development process in Colorado as inclusive as possible, and included representatives of major Colorado companies and legislative leaders on his trips.

However, his need to elevate Colorado's responsiveness for economic opportunities precluded a focused and measured approach to economic development policy. The message within Colorado became muddled and confused. Between November 1986 and July 1990, at least ten state-focused economic development strategic plans, blueprints, and status reports were published in Colorado. These various documents featured the priorities of the Governor and his staff, the legislature, and the business community as they wrestled with the issue of improving Colorado's economy. The documents, and their points-of-view, reflected the fact that economic development policy does not occur in a political vacuum. A review of the documents indicates several commonalities among them. Table 6.1 lists the major reports, their constituency, and dates of publication. To varying degrees, all the documents addressed the following ten issues:

1. Business development, such as the recruitment of new firms, and the expansion and retention of existing firms;
2. Small business issues such as appropriate financing and technical assistance;
3. The rural and agriculture economy;
4. Tourism;
5. Infrastructure, which included transportation issues and water conservation projects such as dams;
6. Education, including preschool, K-12, and higher education, as well as job training;
7. Environmental quality, focusing on air and water quality standards and hazard waste issues;
8. State government organization, reorganization, or both to better respond to economic development opportunities;
9. The role of the private sector in economic development;
10. Tax and finance issues.

Included in some of the reports were issues not normally considered part of the economic development milieu: health care, employee benefit

Table 6.1   Colorado's Economic Development Plans (1986–1989)

Report	Originating Organization	Date Issued
Strategic Plan for Economic Development (Preliminary Draft)	Governor-elect Romer	November 1986
Strategic Plan for Economic Development (Final Report)	Governor Romer	January 1987; one week prior to inauguration
Blueprint for Colorado: A Plan for Growth from the Business Community (Blueprint I)	Colorado Association of Commerce and Industry (CACI)	January 1987; prior to the inauguration
Economic Development: Status Report and Agenda	Department of Local Affairs	June 1987
Plan for a Competitive Colorado	Governor's Office	November 1987
Blueprint II	CACI	January 1988
State of Colorado Program/Finance Report: Economic Development	Office of State Planning and Budgeting	March 1988
Colorado Vision 2000	General Assembly and the private sector	January 1989
Targeted Opportunities for Business Development in Colorado	Office of Economic Development and University of Colorado	April 1989
Blueprint III	CACI	Undated

issues, rehabilitation of criminal offenders, self-sufficiency/welfare reform, intergovernmental cooperation, and the cultural arts. (Interestingly, these ancillary issues were addressed only in the private sector reports—the *Blueprint* reports and *Colorado Vision 2000*.)

None of the reports provided a definition of economic development. Nor did they provide a baseline analysis of the current economic picture other than to note that it was not satisfactory and needed to be improved. Moreover,they did not examine the state's strengths and weaknesses sufficiently enough to achieve widespread consensus. Each report basically reflected the views of its constituencies. Finally, the reports did not delineate the roles of the various key players or stakeholders relative to economic development. Many of the reports mentioned that the private sector should be a "partner" in economic development initiatives and its role ought to be enhanced; and that the legislature needed to approve various funding proposals and statutory changes. However, the respective roles among sectors (public, private, nonprofit) and those within sectors (legislative and executive branches at both the state and local levels) were neither defined nor prescribed. As a result of these omissions, economic development in Colorado often became mired in political competition. This political competition was not so much "partisan" as"institutional."

The Politics of Economic Development

The initial Romer administration document, *Strategic Plan for Economic Development*, appeared as both a preliminary draft and a final report. These initial strategic planning documents were intended to set the tone for the administration's approach to economic development policy. The preliminary draft, published immediately after the election and prior to the inauguration, was "designed to be a starting point" for a series of discussions or "economic summits" with Colorado's top business and community leaders as well as economic development specialists "to produce a very specific strategy for getting Colorado's economy back on track. . . ."[1] The strategic plan outlined thirteen goals for the state's economic revitalization and an organizational structure to accomplish those goals. Among the more significant goals cited was the development of an "economic partnership" between the private sector and state government and increased state and private resources for business development. The final report, published one week prior to Romer's inauguration, summarized the economic summits that had occurred between November and January and outlined a series of specific initiatives clustered into several categories: state government organization, business development within Colorado, small business development, rural development, tourism, and financial institutions.

In addition to the organizational decisions and the initial economic initiatives outlined in the strategic plan, several other issues critical to Colorado's economic future were addressed. These included the construction of the Denver Convention Center, transportation issues, and the roles of K-12 education and job training in economic development.

The timing of the two Romer reports clearly indicated the serious nature of economic development to the governor and his administration. These initial reports attempted to establish the tone of the governor's economic development efforts and raise the visibility of Colorado in terms of business recruitment and development. The effort was designed to be inclusive (that is, obtain the input of a great number and variety of people throughout Colorado) and to outline the organizational approach of state government's role in economic development. Perhaps the most significant factor in the Romer strategic plans was the importance placed on partnerships between the private sector and state government relative to economic development efforts. Such cooperation between business and government had not been pursued previously.

The business community, however, came up with its own strategic plan for economic development. Entitled *Blueprint for Colorado: A Plan for Growth from the Business Community,* the report was published by the Colorado Association of Commerce and Industry (CACI) prior to Romer's inauguration in January 1987. *Blueprint I,* as it came to be called (two others would be published in subsequent years), outlined several initiatives for accelerating economic development and improving job opportunities for Colorado. The report focused on infrastructure issues, education, environmental quality (items not addressed by the Romer documents), state government organization, a role for the private sector in economic development, and tax and finance issues. Issues not addressed by *Blueprint I* that were contained in the Romer documents included business expansion, small businesses, rural and agriculture, and tourism. Basically, the CACI report focused on issues relevant to its membership—primarily large businesses located in the Denver metropolitan area.

The two sets of strategic plans, Romer's and CACI's, served to keep the issue of economic development before the public. However, they also confused the public and ultimately the state legislature about *who* was defining economic development policy for Colorado—the governor or the private sector. Romer's strategic plans were more general, and tended to focus on an activist role for state government under the leadership of the governor. *Blueprint I* was more detailed and specific, calling for 2 percent annual job growth, 175,000 new jobs by 1991, and an unemployment rate 1.5 percent below national levels, and tended to be viewed as the private sector's legislative agenda.

The close timing in the publication of the Romer administration strategic plans and CACI *Blueprints* gave the appearance of jockeying for control over the economic development debate between the public and private sectors. Moreover, within state government, the governor's staff and bureaucrats competed for control of policy-making and resources. Very little discretionary funds were available to use for economic development programs. Traditionally, energy impact funds (taxes collected from oil and gas and mining companies that extracted resources from Colorado), under control of the Department of Local Affairs, were used to finance new programs. While they were intrigued by the new "sexiness" of economic development, the bureaucrats in the department were reluctant to relinquish oversight of these funds to the political appointees now controlling economic development policy. Between November 1986 and April 1987, at least six reorganizations of economic development within state government were proposed. Economic development became a political football with bureaucrats and political appointees competing for possession. Each reorganization sent a new message as to who was controlling economic development policy, a message that tended to confuse not only Coloradans, but also new firms looking to relocate to the state.

An economic development role for the state legislature was virtually ignored. The legislature was primarily viewed as the funding authority for the various programs proposed in the name of economic development. This tended to position legislators as the "heavies" if these programs were not funded. Some of the legislative leadership were included on trips to recruit businesses to Colorado, but when a prospective firm was identified, legislators were excluded from the negotiation process by the governor's staff. If a firm was successfully recruited to the state, the legislature was also prevented from accruing any political credit; that fell solely to the governor.

The plethora of strategic plans and status reports issued by the Romer administration (six of the ten reports noted in table 6.1 were administration documents) coupled with the political infighting between the bureaucrats and political appointees tended to obfuscate priorities. Moreover, not obtaining clear consensus on a baseline—where the state began in terms of economic development—made measurement of success difficult at best. Job creation tended to be the unit of measure for success used by the governor's staff. This measure, by definition, applied primarily to new firms recruited to the state and omitted any assistance for existing companies and small businesses. Thus, the major criticism of Romer's economic development policy was that it leaned heavily toward marketing Colorado to companies that might be willing to relocate, rather than providing assistance to those businesses already in the state.

The Case for a Strategic Approach to Economic Development

In March 1987, the Corporation for Enterprise Development (CfED) published its first "report card" on states' economies, *Making the Grade: The Development Report Card for the States.* The CfED report card used a series of indexes to rate states' economic competitiveness. Colorado rated fairly well: a "B" in the Performance Index, ranked twentieth among states; an "A" in the Business Vitality Index, ranked fifth overall among states; and another "A" in the Capacity Index, with an overall ranking of fourth. However, in the Policy Index, Colorado received a "D," and was ranked thirtieth among the states. This category reflected states' policy strengths in economic development activities, that is, the effectiveness of governance and regulatory policies, tax policies, improved education and research, and assistance to distressed communities.[2] The implication for Colorado was that while its economic performance and vitality and its capacity to grow were all above average to excellent, its policy dearth would not sustain the favorable potential. The lack of sufficient policies resulted from not adequately assessing Colorado's comparative advantage and devising strategies to build on strengths and mitigate weaknesses.

A number of critics within Colorado also noted the lack of specific policies upon which to build the state's sustained economic development policies. In early 1988, Romer was being encouraged to "go beyond cheerleading and develop specific strategies" to improve Colorado's economy.[3] Legislators were lamenting the "mixed signals" they were receiving from an apparently unfocused economic development agenda.[4] In a paper prepared for the Western Governors' Association, economists Weinstein and Gross noted "that new economic and political realities facing the West call for revised approaches in stimulating business and economic development."[5] These revised approaches should focus on strategies that foster "internally-generated economic development . . . in particular, emphasis should be placed on business retention, job creation through expansion of existing firms, and the encouragement of new business formation."[6]

Barriers to Strategic Action

Economic development is a wealth creation *process.* It is not, in and of itself, job creation. This "subtle but important distinction"[7] is one not always understood by those charged with making public policy. Moreover, because policymakers are driven primarily by political expediency, they have a tendency to confuse the creation of jobs with economic development. As Vaughan and associates note, developing effective economic strategies for a state rests on the ability to identify the "functions that it can plan, manage, and coordinate efficiently and then do them well. Expanding its activities into those areas where the state does not have a comparative advantage—however well intentioned—will fail to achieve these objectives and will make the state less effective in carrying out its basic duties."[8] The key, then, is for a state to identify its comparative advantage.

Perhaps Governor Romer's most serious flaw in his economic development efforts has been in not identifying, or obtaining agreement on, Colorado's comparative advantage. Not one of the six major policy documents issued by his economic development staff focused on identifying and capitalizing on the state's comparative advantages.

Romer and his advisors felt that immediate action was essential to improve Colorado's economy. However, this bias for action precluded a focused, strategic approach to economic development policy for Colorado. The marketing of the state—creating the perception that Colorado was "open for business"—took precedence as an economic development priority. None of the strategic plans noted in table 6.1 attempted to assess: Colorado's strengths and weaknesses; economic trends and their impacts upon the state; leadership issues; inventories of resources to implement selected strategies; efforts to match resources to strategic objectives; or other states' strategies. The absence of these assessments meant that the *context* for action by the Romer administration was not well understood. Thus, no front-end agreement was obtained among the various stakeholders regarding the priorities that needed to be addressed. The key decision makers had not agreed early on in the process what the measures of success would be for the state's economic development efforts. Thus, by default, job creation became the measure of success. This put the Romer administration in the position of applying most of its limited resources toward marketing and recruiting at the expense of small business assistance and firms already in Colorado.

The major lesson learned from Colorado's approach is that the publication of strategic planning documents does not guarantee strategic action. Rather, a well-defined and agreed-on *process* that addresses a state's strengths and weaknesses, analyzes the current economic picture and future trends, and focuses resources and activities is critical to the success of a state's strategic approach to economic development.

Notes

1. Roy Romer, *Strategic Plan for Economic Development: Preliminary Draft* (Nov. 1986).
2. Corporation for Enterprise Development, *Making the Grade: The Development Report Card for the States* (Washington, D.C.: Corporation for Enterprise Development, 1987), p. 12.
3. Jeffrey Leib, "After the Cheerleading, Specific Boot-Strapping Strategies Crucial," *Denver Post*, Jan. 24, 1988.
4. John Diaz and Jeffrey Roberts, "Romer Plants Policy Seeds: Harvest Uncertain," *Denver Post*, Jan. 24, 1988.
5. Bernard L. Weinstein and Harold T. Gross, *The Western Economy in Transition: Nature, Causes, and Implications* (Denver, Colo.: Western Governors' Association, 1986), pp. vi-vii.
6. Ibid.
7. Roger J. Vaughan, Robert Pollard and Barbara Dryer, *The Wealth of States: The Political Economy of State Development* (Washington, D.C.: Council of State Planning Agencies, 1985), pp. 1-3.
8. Ibid., pp. 1-7.

SEVEN

DESIGNING SUCCESSFUL STATE RURAL DEVELOPMENT STRATEGIES

David W. Sears, John M. Redman, Richard L. Gardner, and Stephen J. Adams

IN 1990, we partcipated in a Rural Policy Academy that was orchestrated by the Council of Governors' policy advisors. This academy brought together top-level policy teams from ten states. We watched the teams struggle with the substantive and organizational questions of developing and implementing rural development policy. We believed that it would be useful to put down, in a logical and clearly articulated form, the key issues that such state policymakers must face. This chapter is our attempt to do that.[1]

For most Americans, the concept of "rural" brings to mind images of agriculture—cows grazing in open meadows and corn lined up in neat rows as far as the eye can see. The true shape of the rural United States is hardly so homogeneous. A careful look at rural America will reveal not just farmlands, but also mines and oil wells, woodlands, industrial centers, government facilities, exurban subdivisions, resorts and retirement communities. Within this diversity, however, certain common features are widely shared.

The first commonality is low density. Rural America is that part of the nation that is populated sparsely.[2] Historically, rural economies have been built upon a foundation of natural resources, including farmland, timber, and minerals, as well as attractive landscapes. Even the manufacturing and service industries in rural areas are often directly tied into this natural resource base. This strong linkage to a fixed natural resource base is another commonality that cuts across the diverse array of rural communities.

Many rural areas are characterized by relatively poor performance on a variety of economic and social indicators. Frequently, job growth, earnings per job, average income levels, educational levels, skill levels, and indices of public health are lower than in metro areas. In addition, when compared to metropolitan areas, rural economies often are more narrowly specialized, possess lower quality infrastructure, provide less access to common public services, and offer fewer cultural amenities.

While rural economic conditions are often poorer than urban conditions, rural places frequently have some relative advantages. The attractive rural landscape and/or lower pressure rural lifestyle may appeal to tourists and retirees, as well as to commuters who wish to work in the city or its suburbs but live in lower density areas. Low population density may, in addition, make rural areas more suitable for a handful of somewhat undesirable activities such as prisons, waste disposal facilities, and electric generating operations. The generally lower wages of rural areas continue to appeal to a range of lower skill, labor-intensive manufacturing industries. Some rural places with relatively low wages but moderately skilled/educated workers have been successful in attracting some skilled or semi-skilled service functions traditionally performed in metro areas, for example, accounting, telemarketing, and claims processing.

The balance between problems and opportunities varies dramatically across rural areas of the United States. In some rural areas, only an optimist or imaginative local leader can see much in the way of economic opportunities. At the other extreme, in a minority of rural communities, the major problem is controlling and/or adapting to the economic growth that is occurring.

"Economic development" is a term that can be defined in a variety of ways. Part of the struggle in coming to grips with rural economic development is deciding how broadly to focus the effort. A narrow definition might include those activities intended to move a region toward full employment. A broader definition might focus on the attainment of a minimum income level for each local resident. Still more broadly, economic development can be aimed at improving not only employment and income levels but also the physical and cultural attributes of local life; thus, some of the results of economic development might include a cleaner environment, access to a broader range of health care services, and improved access to the arts. Under the broadest definition, economic development could be seen as an ongoing process of building and maintaining local and regional institutions (business, educational, health, transportation) which not only generates an acceptable quality of life today but also promotes continued and/or enhanced viability in the future.

For more than a decade, the federal government has not played a leading, activist role in promoting economic development. In response, many states have broadened their own development efforts. This passing of leadership from the federal to the state level has been a major impetus for greater state activity in rural development in recent years.

The Rationale for State Leadership in Rural Development

Given the combination of shrinking resources and expanding demands on state government, a convincing argument must be made for state involvement in rural economic development. This argument has two interconnected components—first, those reasons for public sector involvement in the state's economy in general and, second, those reasons for devoting special attention to the rural portion of the economy. A substantial and well-known body of literature exists to provide a rationale for public sector intervention in the economy at large (for recent examples, see Bartik, 1990, and Eisner, 1991); we will not reiterate that justification here. Rather, we will focus on the second component.

Perhaps the strongest argument for focusing on a state's rural economy is to improve rural-urban equity. As noted earlier, numerous disparities—on a variety of economic and social indicators—between rural and urban areas exist and have been increasing over the past decade. In many states, the emergence of a dual economy, with severely lagging rural regions, can serve as a strong justification for state involvement in the rural economy—in order to facilitate a more even distribution of economic opportunities across the state.

A second justification for a rural focus is the existence of rural-urban linkages; because of such links, the state's urban areas may feel directly the impacts of rural problems. Such transmission of problems may take place in two ways: through migration or through market linkages. Rural problems of low skill levels and high unemployment, for example, may become urban problems through migration from the state's rural to its urban areas. In addition, rural-urban migration will increase congestion, and its associated costs, in the state's urban regions. Through urban-rural linkages within the state, problems of market failure in the rural economy can exert an indirect drag on the metro economy; this might occur, for example, through slow production or poor quality goods or services sent by rural suppliers to urban firms.

Maintenance of existing rural facilities may be important but difficult. Thus, a third justification holds that it is more efficient to make full use of fixed investments (e.g., schools, roads, municipal water and sewer systems, retail stores) already in place in rural areas than to abandon these. An effort that is made to help rural communities will thus result in a fuller use of these investments. Another part of this argument holds that urbanites visiting rural areas (e.g., on vacation) will find it efficient to have key services (e.g., food, lodging, auto repairs) on hand.

Preservation of a rural "way of life" is a fourth justification. The premise here is that there is a different lifestyle that is found in many rural communities; the attributes of this lifestyle include neighborliness, a slower pace, a focus on "family" and "traditional values," an appreciation of the land and "nature," and a strong work ethic. Regardless of their accuracy, these are perceptions that many people—both urban and rural—accept. Building upon this premise of a special rural way of life, and the cited indicators of relatively severe rural economic problems, the argument is made that state attention to rural areas is needed to help preserve this "endangered" lifestyle.

The four preceding arguments for justifying special state attention to rural regions follow in large part from the relatively poor economic performance of most rural areas when compared with metro areas. A fifth justification is that these areas are, in some basic characteristics, simply different from urban areas. For instance, beyond equity considerations, the very low population density of rural areas often requires different service delivery mechanisms (e.g., for health care, public transportation, job training) than urban areas.

A sixth argument that might be made for focusing attention on rural areas within a state is to improve the efficiency of the state's economy. Here, public sector intervention would be justified as a means for overcoming or ameliorating a market failure[3]; these failures will decrease the efficiency of the overall economy. In some states, market failure in rural areas may be so much more severe than in metro areas that special attention paid to correcting these failings in rural areas may have particularly good payoffs in terms of improving the efficiency of the state's overall economy. The relative efficiency gains from devoting a state's resources to rural, rather than urban, development activities, however, will clearly vary from state to state.

Organizing for Rural Development—An Overview

If key players in a state government all sat down one day and asked themselves what they could or should do to stimulate rural economic development in the state, they would have to make a number of choices about how to organize the effort. Much current state government activity likely does, in fact, contribute to rural development, but was originally conceived without benefit of an overall rural development strategy. However many rural-related programs a state may have today, it might usefully gather key players together to think about the best way to further organize and/or reorganize its resources.[4] There is no single "right" way for a state to organize itself to carry out rural economic development. But, there are certainly "more promising" and "less promising" ways. The state's specific economic, social, cultural, organizational, and political context will provide opportunities and set constraints that must be taken into account. In brief, what works well in one state might not in another.

When a state is ready to begin organizing itself for rural economic development, at least eleven key choices must be made. If these choices are not made explicitly, they will be made implicitly. We have divided these eleven choices into three major categories: setting the basic ground rules for planning, establishing relationships with other key players, and setting the basic ground rules for implementation. These choices are discussed below.[5]

Setting the Ground Rules for Planning Rural Development

Goal-Setting

Several of the Rural Development Policy Academy teams spent a good deal of energy attempting to develop a "vision" of change they would like to see in their rural areas. As simple as this activity might seem, it is not always easy to gain agreement on a single goal or vision. Some key state policymakers may be able to clearly articulate objectives for specific programs in their agecies, but may be so focused on these programs that they have no clear concept of an overall rural development goal and how other agencies or programs might fit in.

There are two main advantages of a single explicitly stated goal. First, its existence makes it easier for all to see what specific state actions will help in achieving the goal—and which won't. Second, the goal development process is likely to force interdisciplinary, crosscutting discussions—a process that cannot help but improve the quality of policy analysis and forge interagency ties as the participants ask tough questions of their peers and respond with thoughtful answers, and as similarities and differences among team members are better defined.

The main disadvantage of a single overarching goal is that the process of establishing such a goal may involve battles among interests with ardently held perspectives. The outcome of such battles may be only a weak consensus on the goal, increased animosity among the protagonists and a sense of frustration that so much time was spent with so little benefit. Such an outcome becomes more likely the more each participant's perspective is colored by his or her position within the state government and a conscious or unconscious desire to protect agency "turf."

In a variety of circumstances, then, achievement of widespread agreement on an explicitly stated rural development goal/vision simply may not be worth the effort. It is critical, however, that at least a minimal level of consensus on a shared vision for rural development emerge from the discussion, even if that vision is somewhat abstract and the consensus is only implicit.

Links among Programs

A state might choose a comprehensive approach to rural economic development. Under a comprehensive approach, major aspects of rural development (e.g., health care, education and training, infrastructure investment, resource management, environmental protection, job development) would be considered in relation to each other and melded into a single strategy.

The alternative would be to choose an approach in which separate strategies are developed for different aspects of rural development on an as-needed basis. For instance, under the piecemeal approach, the state might one year develop an education strategy in response to a court case mandating greater equity among school districts and then in the following year develop a rural health care strategy in response to the closing of several small rural hospitals.

The advantage of the comprehensive approach is that interrelationships among various activities can be worked through in a systematic fashion, and a variety of ways to achieve objectives of rural development can be more easily considered. The disadvantage of the comprehensive approach is that power—and thus decision-making—in state governments is often disaggregated into fairly autonomous fiefdoms, making the comprehensive approach intellectually satisfying but politically frustrating and/or irrelevant.

Breadth

State policymakers may choose to develop a separate rural development strategy, or they may choose to incorporate activities aimed at enhancing rural development into a unitary state economic development plan.

With the unitary approach, rural development does not get put to the side or ignored in making key decisions about the overall state economy. In addition, the linkages—which may often be of prime importance—between the state's metro and nonmetro economies can be more readily acknowledged and built upon under a unitary approach. The disadvantage of the unitary approach is that it may overlook the unique needs and problems of the state's rural areas. Many states may choose a compromise approach; under such a compromise, the major pieces of the state's rural development actions (e.g., training and education) could be integrated into an overall state development plan, while some uniquely rural problems (e.g., health care facilities and services for low density areas) might be handled outside that plan.

People or Places

Rural development can emphasize "people"—as in: "The problem is that rural families have to live on extremely low incomes." Or, rural development can emphasize "place"—as in: "The problem is out-migration." Sometimes a rural development strategy that attempts to improve prospects for people will also improve prospects for places,[6] but often these objectives are in conflict. The most stark example of this conflict can be seen in state efforts to improve the education and skill levels of rural children and adults. Such an investment will improve the prospects for rural people, but as a result of these improved prospects (i.e., an ability to qualify for more highly skilled and more highly paid jobs), possibilities for mobility will be increased and the likelihood of outmigration of "the best and the brightest" from nonvibrant rural places may be increased.

A state government will want to think carefully about whether to focus on improving prospects for people or for places in its rural development efforts. Since the welfare of individuals is the presumed ultimate aim of all government activities, an emphasis on people is most directly related to this end. On the other hand, the advantage of an emphasis on places is that this meshes best with what most people envision as rural development—an attempt to protect or enhance the economic viability of rural communities. An overall state rural development strategy may, of course, include some components that focus on people (e.g., job training programs for rural residents) and other components that emphasize places (e.g., upgrading wastewater treatment facilities in rural communities).

Establishing Relationships with Other Key Players

Federal Government

Should the state government attempt to coordinate its rural development activities with those of the federal government? Several of the states participating in the federally stimulated pilot State Rural Development Councils are hopeful that such coordination will be a primary mechanism for achieving the state's rural development goals.

The advantage of such coordination is that the state's limited resources can be stretched further—as the state can choose to focus on plugging those holes not covered by federal resources, or the state can attempt to pull (or push) federal resources into specific areas that the state can't handle. On the other hand, the time and energy devoted to coordination may sap scarce resources and produce few benefits. Or, the "coordinating partners" may not be fully committed to coordination. Under the federal pilot State Rural Development Council effort, federal agencies are being prodded to coordinate with each other and with state agencies; but the on-the-ground results across all states and across all federal agencies over the next several years remain to be seen.

Other Governments

We believe that states will continue to play, into the foreseeable future, a central role. Thus, our focus is on the state government. But, we do not see the state as the only player. We recognize that others have resources (goods, services, knowledge) to bring to the table. In fact, the state may find that a critical piece of its rural development activity is soliciting and utilizing input on goals and activities from a variety of players from outside state government, including local, regional, and tribal governments. Another key issue, then, is the extent to which the state will attempt to coordinate its activities with those of these other players. The advantages and disadvantages of a high degree of coordination are similar to those just discussed in terms of state-federal coordination.

Communities, Clusters, and Regions

As part of preparation of a rural economic development strategy for the state, a choice will have to be made about the appropriate level of program implementation. The state can choose the community (e.g., town or village) as the appropriate unit; then, sewer grants, for example, might be made to individual localities. Another possibility is that the state can choose the cluster of communities (i.e., in rural areas, several nearby small communities would voluntarily join together to form a "cluster") as the appropriate unit for implementation of programs/ services; then, sewer grants might be made to the cluster, with the cluster then given the responsibility to decide how best to use the grant monies within the several communities of the cluster.[7] Or, the multi-county region could be chosen as the appropriate unit.[8]

Allocating resources to individual communities will enable the state to consider the unique characteristics of specific rural localities. The advantage of implementation at a regional level is that conflicts among individual localities will have to be handled within the region—perhaps leading to greater cooperation, and a more efficient use of the state's limited resources.

Setting the Ground Rules for Implementation

Targeting

Another key choice that a state must make is whether to target its resources, and, if so, how. Targeting involves allocating certain state resources to localities or sectors or individuals with particular characteristics that make them especially attractive or worthy recipients.[9] The opposite—untargeted—approach would be to allocate resources evenly throughout the state, or at least its rural portion, on the basis of some "neutral" factor such as population.

If targeting is chosen, there are several ways to allocate state resources. The state might choose to target geographic areas or industrial sectors with weak economic performance; in many states, such targeting would have a strong rural emphasis. Alternatively, the state might target areas or sectors with good economic opportunities.[10] Another basis for targeting could be to focus on particularly severe or clear market failures. Other bases for targeting are possible; size, need, and evidence of strong entrepreneurial behavior are examples. Finally, in order to get the most bang for the buck, the state might target its resources to communities with a strong and well-administered local service delivery mechanism.

An extreme approach to targeting is "triage"; under triage, all resources for a particular program would be allocated to a select set of communities or industrial sectors. For instance, triage might involve dividing the state's rural communities into those that will do well without any assistance from the state, those that are unlikely to survive (i.e., those that will literally turn into ghost towns, as well as those that will become over the years decreasingly viable as economic entities), and those that are on the borderline (i.e., those where some assistance from the state is likely to make a substantial difference in the survival rate). If a state were to use the triage approach, growth-oriented assistance (e.g., infrastructure development, business modernization assistance, new business development, industrial recruitment, training for skill upgrading) might be targeted exclusively on communities with characteristics thought to be associated with the borderline group. Those judged unlikely to survive might not only receive fewer resources, but these resources would be dedicated primarily to worker and community adjustment (e.g., assistance to consolidate service delivery, job search assistance with appropriate training, relocation assistance, extended income support). No special assistance would be provided to those communities judged to possess a strong economy.

The advantage of targeting resources is that, if the targeting criteria are thoughtfully selected and carefully implemented, the state's limited resources should go further in achieving the state's rural development goals. The disadvantage of targeting is that such thoughtful selection may be politically difficult to carry out; discrimination in favor of certain groups or regions can also be seen as discrimination against certain other groups or regions. In addition, little or no evidence may exist to support the contention that a particular form of targeting will better achieve the state's rural development goals than no targeting. Triage is simply an extreme case of targeting; thus, its advantages and disadvantages are similar, but more pronounced. In short, some degree of targeting of the state's resources is a compromise between explicit triage and making no differentiation among the prospects of the state's communities. Many states will find that such a compromise is appropriate.

Service Delivery Structure

How to make each dollar of state resources go as far as it can go is always important, but is particularly critical when federal resources available for a broad range of development activities are diminishing, as has been the case for more than a decade. A key issue to be confronted, then, is how best to structure the delivery of services for rural development. A growing number of service delivery models are emanating from the states. Four basic models are presented here.

Most public programs rely on the first model—"direct service delivery" by designated public agencies, for example, job training by the state's employment and training agency, and education of children by the local school district. An advantage of this model is that the public sector maintains direct control over the quantity and quality of services delivered. A second advantage is clear accountability—clients of programs will understand that the state government should receive the "credit" for good service or "blame" for poor service. A disadvantage that is frequently cited is bureaucratic inflexibility and inefficiency.

Recently, some states have attempted to circumvent the first model by placing control of resources in the hands of those receiving the service while simultaneously introducing competition among service providers; this is a second model. The major assumption underlying this "competitive" model is that efficiency and outcomes can be enhanced by diffusing demand and making providers compete. Because these efforts are so recent, however, there is little empirical evidence to show that they do indeed improve program performance significantly without inadvertently producing additional problems.

During the 1970s, a third model emerged. Under this model, public resources are stretched by requiring private matching funds. For example, a local revolving loan fund might be established only if local private resources are obtained to match state dollars. Strong advantages of this approach are that private money is leveraged to help achieve public goals, there is a greater confidence that the public activity is responding to private market signals, and strong political support for the service is provided by the participating private sector actors. A disadvantage of this approach (as with the first two models) is that overall activity levels are still limited by the level of public resources available; thus, many eligible and interested clients (e.g., of job training) may not access the service.

A fourth model removes the state directly from service or resource provision after an initial effort to build self-sustaining private institutional capacity. Conceptually, building effective, self-sustaining, private institutions to accomplish private goals (e.g., the creation of flexible manufacturing networks to enhance the competitiveness of a state's industrial base) is an ideal solution to the service delivery dilemma. It is yet unclear, however, where this model applies and how its effectiveness might vary from problem to problem.

Local Use of State Funds

To promote rural development, the state government is likely to have a variety of resources available. These resources will include financial resources to purchase goods and services (e.g., bridges and training programs) and expert assistance that can be provided to localities. The state can maintain tight or loose control over these resources. Under tight control, the state will make decisions on the detailed allocation of its resources. Under loose control, the state will send funds to localities as block grants, permitting the communities to spend the resources as they see fit to promote economic development (within the constraints of a few overall guidelines such as nondiscrimination and environmental protection).

A middle-of-the-road compromise is the "smorgasbord" approach. Under the smorgasbord approach, the state will carefully design an array of programs, each of which will (presumably) be useful to some (though probably not all) communities, and each locality can choose from this menu those programs that it believes will be most useful for its economic development goals. Under the smorgasbord approach, the locality may be required to have some sort of training that would assist it in becoming an "informed consumer." In addition, the state would probably give each locality a cap on the total amount of state resources that it can tap through these programs.

The advantage of tight control is that, for a state that "knows what's needed" to promote rural development, implementation is straight-forward and not muddled by getting localities involved. The advantage of loose control is that those closest to the scene of the action—the localities—can select those activities that they believe will be most likely to stimulate rural development without interference from the state; these communities will feel a pride of ownership in the implemented projects. The advantage of the smorgasbord approach is that it permits both the state and localities to offer useful insights on the best way to carry out rural development in the state.

Local Capacity Building

The economic development literature in recent years has devoted considerable energy to delineating the problem of "local capacity building." Capacity building is aimed at developing knowledgeable local leadership that can respond to, and even create, opportunities for economic development.

At one extreme, the state could take an active role in local capacity building. In this active role, the state could provide the resources to enable localities to build their intellectual and organizational capacity to carry out economic development—and the state would actively encourage communities to take advantage of state programs (e.g., training programs for local leaders on how to organize and carry out strategic planning for economic development) to build this capacity. Or, the state's role could be more passive. The state could design a program to build local capacity, but only communities that taking the initiative to seek out the program would participate. (At the extreme, of course, the state might choose to have no program of local capacity building.)

The advantage of an active approach to local capacity building is that this can be meshed neatly with a targeting approach, if the state has chosen to target its resources. On the other hand, a passive approach can be seen as an implicit targeting approach—only those communities with a certain amount of initiative will receive the state's capacity building program.

Some Suggestions for States

There are no universally "correct" answers to the questions posed in the previous sections; in that sense, the issues discussed here present real choices. In contrast, we feel that the following nine suggestions may prove useful to many states as they attempt to promote rural economic development.

Build upon previous work. All states in the United States have carried out some rural development activities, and all states have done some thinking about rural development. In any state, a variety of documents will be available which lays out previous research and thinking on some or all aspects of rural development. Not all of this previous work will provide useful information or insights. Nevertheless, a state which is about to launch a major effort on rural development would be foolish not to look carefully at previous work, and to draw from that work whatever may be useful.

Conduct detailed analysis of economy. It is tempting to respond to rural economic problems by jumping immediately into action. While some immediate action may be warranted, and in the long run may prove to be beneficial, actions that are carefully grounded in good solid analysis of the state's economic situation will have a much better chance of achieving long-term benefits than actions that are merely quick reactions to crises. At the very least the state should have a basic understanding of the key elements of its economy. For each important sector in the state's economy (as well as for potentially important sectors), the state needs to have an understanding of how that sector is positioned in the domestic and world economy and how that position limits or offers expanded opportunities. Key questions to be addressed include these: Who are the competitors? What are they doing? How are they different (or the same) in terms of technology, management, investment levels, wage levels, workforce quality and training, product development, and public support? How are markets and technology changing? What are the bottlenecks faced by the sector in developing, producing and marketing new and existing products and services? What market failures (we list eight of them in note 3) are constraining development possibilities in the sector?

Build upon the existing economic base. In analyzing economic structure and prosperity, it is easy to focus heavily on new kinds of activities, for example, biotechnology, boutique raspberries, robotics. But, often a state will do well to do what it has been doing in recent years, but to do it differently. This is not to say that a state shouldn't consider doing some things, even lots of things, that are new; only that the first question to ask is: "To what extent does the existing industrial base offer an opportunity to significantly upgrade rural skills and wages?" Once a state is satisfied with that answer, it then can go on to consider what new activities might realistically be expected to assist in the upgrading.

Conduct an institutional scan. In any state an array of institutions—in both the public and private sectors—might contribute to the development and implementation of a rural development strategy. A state will want, at a minimum, to have a checklist of these institutions in order to be sure that the critical ones are involved in the strategy development process. Pertinent questions about the candidate institutions include: Which ones are currently active in rural development in the state? Which are effective? Which have potentially useful resources (including funds and skills)? Which are powerful? Whose support or opposition might make or break a rural development scheme?

Create partnerships. To carry out the type of analysis and strategy development suggested above, it is crucial to create partnerships with knowledgeable private sector actors/organizations.[11] In many states, the individuals and organizations with the most detailed understanding of what is going on in a given industry will be those in the industry itself.

Private sector investment will also help prevent the state from proposing specific policies/programs which are not well-targeted to actual needs or which are, in fact, counterproductive. In addition, a rural development strategy that is developed by the state in isolation—without knowledgeable input from the private sector—is less likely to gain a broad base of political support.

Be politically realistic and astute. The success of a rural development strategy will rely as much upon its political support as its operational design. In most states, politically skilled "insiders" will be an essential part of any team that successfully moves to address rural development. Having the governor (or key staff) and the legislative leadership as central players in the process of putting together the state's rural development strategy will help ensure that political realism will prevail. Agency participation must not be just "token" representation; rather, it is important that key agency heads be fully committed.

Political astuteness is also important—this involves identifying unique political windows of opportunity, and then taking advantage of such opportunities. These windows could include an economic crisis, a natural disaster, a one-time budget surplus, or an impending reapportionment of political districts. The key element here is getting the poiltical experts fully involved when developing plans for implementation.

Establish priorities. Once several interested and committed players have come together to work on the state's rural development issues, there will be a movement to consolidate the identified problems and proposals into an all-inclusive "laundry list." Establishment of such a list will often be an important intermediate step in the process of developing a state strategy, but it should not be viewed as the final step. If the state is to have an important role in shaping the rural economy, priorities must be established among the various actions that the state might undertake to stimulate its rural economy. Only in this way will limited resources be focused upon the actions that are seen as absolutely critical.

Limit the immediate objectives. Yet another temptation will be to focus attention and energy on the achievement of broad long-term goals. Given the political and economic realities faced in most states, this would be a soul-satisfying but impractical way to go about doing business. Few long-term victories can be won without a number of short-term victories along the way to build and sustain momentum and support for rural development. Thus, the best approach would seem to be to keep the long-term vision in mind, but to focus immediate attention upon limited and achievable short-term objectives.

Build in evaluation—And use it. Over the course of years, and decades, there will be ebbs and flows in the resources and interest devoted to rural development. But no matter how successful this year's strategy may be in addressing the state's rural development problems and opportunities, there will be a need for more work in future years. In addition, since regional economic structures are in constant flux, strategies that are successful today may no longer be appropriate at some point in the future. Therefore, the state should build an evaluation component into its rural development strategy. The evaluation should be used to think about whether various pieces of the state's rural development approach make sense exactly as implemented or might be modified to become even more effective.

A Final Word

Over the past decade, leadership for rural development in America has gravitated to state government. As the overall state of the rural economy in the United States has deteriorated since the late 1970s, the need for solid workable rural development strategies has increased. Thus, the importance of the states' activities to stimulate rural economic development is greater than it has been at any time in recent history, and the challenges are perhaps more daunting than before. Despite the enormity of the task, states can make a real difference in this critical policy area.

Notes

1. This chapter is a streamlined version of a more expansive paper. It is short on examples, in-depth explanations, and justifications of the points we made in the earlier version. Should a reader wish to see the longer paper, please write to David W. Sears, Economic Research Service, Room 324M, 1301 New York Ave. NW, Washington DC 20005-4788.

2. Four types of places in the United States can be imagined: (a) large cities and their adjacent suburbs, (b) small towns and other urbanized areas not part of any metropolitan area, (c) sparsely populated

areas inside the boundaries of metropolitan areas, and (d) sparsely populated areas outside metropolitan areas. Under no definition would the first type of place be called rural. And under all definitions, the last type of place would be rural. The conceptually "in between" places—the second and third types—are those that will be handled differently under different definitions.

3. At least eight types of market failures are of relevance here: unemployment, underemployment, underinvestment in research, key capital shortages, key information shortages, undervaluing of agglomeration economies, undervaluing of positive externalities (such as the downstream benefits of soil conservation or wastewater processing investments), and underinvestment in merit goods (such as education, training, and health care) that provide positive social benefits. See Bartik (1990) for a discussion of most of these failures.

4. The remainder of this paper is based heavily upon our recent experiences with the 1990 Rural Development Policy Academy, organized by the Council of Governors Policy Advisors, an affiliate the National Governors Association; it is based to a lesser extent upon our observation of the federal government's State Rural Development Council initiative (which was instituted in late 1990). The academy brought together teams of top-level policymakers from each of ten states (AR, CA, IA, ME, MI, MO, MS, ND, PA, WY) to facilitate the development and implementation of individual state rural development strategies; Mark Popovich was the Academy's project director. The federal initiative seeks to promote close state/federal coordination in the planning and implementation of rural development activities within each of eight pilot states (KS, ME, MS, OR, SC, SD, TX, WA).

5. A "final" decision never has to be made on any of these eleven choices. Each choice is subject to later reevaluation. Over time, it is likely that a number of the choices made will be modified—some once and some several times.

6. An example of a specific approach that will contribute substantially to the achievement of both people and place objectives is the provision of rural public transit; such transportation will broaden the job opportunities of carless rural residents while permitting them to live in their hometowns.

7. Clustering of communities may make less sense in the more sparsely settled states of the western half of the United States than it does farther east, where most communities are relatively close to neighboring places.

8. The state does not have to make the same choice for every aspect of rural development. Sewer grants could be allocated to communities,

while decisions about solid waste disposal could be made at a regional level; a physician loan program aimed at enticing more doctors into remote rural locations might be administered at the state level.

9. When we speak of targeting, we are not implying that the state would necessarily focus all of its resources from a particular program on a few geographic areas or industrial sectors. Targeting may also involve focusing an uneven proportion of resources on a few areas or sectors but not to the total exclusion of other areas or sectors.

10. For instance, the state might choose to put its limited resources into those areas or sectors likely to produce the highest marginal return on investment.

11. We explicitly discuss partnerships with the private sector (including nonprofit organizations) here. We think that state government partnerships with federal, local, regional, and tribal governments are also often crucial; however, we discussed those relationships earlier.

PART THREE

Local Government Issues and Economic Development

INSTITUTIONAL POWER AND THE ART OF THE DEAL: AN ANALYSIS OF MUNICIPAL DEVELOPMENT POLICY ADOPTIONS

Richard C. Feiock and James C. Clingermayer

AMERICAN CITIES have pursued various kinds of economic development ever since the founding of the nation. Yet not all cities have been equally diligent in seeking the benefits that are sometimes promised to those governments that adopt particular policies designed to lead to business relocations and additional investment in existing enterprises. Some of the cities that have sought to pursue these policies have been unable to get their proposals past the planning stage.

We propose that one of the primary determinants of a community's decision to pursue a specific form of development policy or strategy is the political-institutional environment of that city. Among the arrangements that shape this environment are the institutions championed by the municipal reform movement, including nonpartisan, at-large elections, weak mayors, and unelected but presumably professional and expert city managers. The nature of a city's institutions encourages particular kinds of behavior and, in fact, encourages particular kinds of people to participate in local politics. These factors, rather than simply economic circumstances or demographic characteristics, can encourage city decision makers to make use of the instruments of economic development policy.

If our argument is correct, we must conclude that certain kinds of cities find themselves favorably suited to make use of policy instruments that many other cities would like to employ, but which they may have considerable difficulty implementing. Particular kinds of institutional characteristics seem to favor these policy instruments. In the long run, we may see those who favor these policy instruments begin to favor such institutional arrangements.

In the first section we describe the advent of the institutions of the municipal reform movement and discuss the implications that reformism has had for recruitment of both elected and unelected officials and for the general "accessibility" of city government. We claim there that development policies, which have uncertain effects upon actual investment decisions, may be adopted in less reformed cities simply because of their political attractiveness. In the next section, we discuss some of the skills and institutional authority that the pursuit of particular development policies may require. We suggest that less reformed governments may lack the organizational capacity to implement easily several kinds of development policy instruments. A third major section describes an empirical test of the proposition that form of government affects the adoption of five development policies widely used in the 1970s and '80s. The analysis also examines two different, competing explanations, one which focuses upon the fiscal stress or "need" for investment in the city, the other which focuses upon the presence of certain organized groups and interests that may be likely to join (or oppose) a pro-growth coalition. The implications of this analysis for local government institutions are discussed in a final section.

Insulated Government, Development Policy, and the "Politics of Announcement"

Much about the municipal reform movement is controversial and subject to heated debate, but what is clear is that one purpose of the recommendations of the municipal reformers was to insulate city government from the presumably harmful influences of old-fashioned, machine politics. The manipulations of political parties were to be thwarted through the use of nonpartisan ballots and limitations upon patronage. The parochialism of ward politics was to be eliminated by requiring council members to be elected at-large, from the city as a whole. Empire-building by ambitious mayors was to be prevented by weakening the office of the mayor and by placing central administrative responsibilities in the hands of a professional city manager who would answer only to the council as a whole, just as a corporate chief executive officer would be responsive to a board of directors. Whether the adoption of these reformist arrangements brought about the decline of machine politics or whether they were just a consequence of that decline is subject to question, but what is clear is that styles of politics and policy making changed with the advent of these new institutions (see, for example, Lineberry and Fowler, 1967; Engstrom and McDonald, 1986; Cassel, 1986).

What many critics of reformed institutions have suggested is that in insulating city government from the evils of machine politics, reformers had separated local government from the citizens whom it was intended to serve. Citizens with little education or information about candidates could no longer look to party labels as a voting cue. Families with problems with city services could no longer expect much help from their council representative, since bureaucracies were centralized under the authority of an unelected professional usually lacking long-term ties to the community, let alone the neighborhood where the service problem was located. Different sorts of people were recruited to both elected office and bureaucratic positions. Local party service became less relevant in elections, while professional credentials and membership in esteemed civic organizations became more valued. For many recruited to office in this way, government service (particularly in elected posts) was a temporary and part-time obligation, not a long-term commitment or potential career choice. Hence, both elected officials and civil servants saw little incentive to bend to the demands of constituents, but instead made decisions based upon personal conviction, professional norms, or input from individuals in high status positions who spoke their language and shared much of their experience.

Lacking a strong mayor, policy making became a product of discussions within the council with little central leadership or initiation of proposals. Deals could not easily be hammered out within the council or between city government or outside actors, such as private firms or the federal government, since no elected official had the formal authority to negotiate on the part of the city or thwart alternatives (through a veto, if necessary) that would break apart coalitions on the council.

In such an environment, we should expect policy making in general to be a relatively slow moving process, with decisive action difficult to accomplish, and with much of the policy initiative displayed, not by elected officials, but by prominent community groups, business firms, other governments, or the city manager. Since elected officials in reformed cities are, in general, less interested in long-term political careers and have a larger, more diffuse set of constituents, they need not worry as much about the political fallout of their policy decisions. The policies they pursue are those that are pleasing to themselves and to prominent people whose support is believed to be necessary to keep the city running smoothly. This means that the policies that elected officials adopt need not be particularly popular. They need not be programs that can be presented on the soapbox for the consumption of the masses.

While this may seem undesirable from the standpoint of maintaining electoral accountability or popular control of government, it does mean that politicians in reformed city governments have little incentive to engage in "symbolic" policy making that has little substantive importance but which gives the public the impression that great and wondrous things are being done. This is significant because many local public policies, including many economic development incentives, are often considered of dubious value in affecting regional relocations of firms, aiding in the creation of new businesses, or in expanding employment within existing enterprises (see Wasylenko, 1981; Fisher, 1985). For this reason, some scholars have argued that municipal development policies are often adopted, not because they are particularly effective, but because they offer opportunities for elected officials to claim that they are doing something for their constituents and the city as a whole. When a firm locates a plant within the city limits and, in doing so, accepts a public subsidy, mayors and council members who supported the subsidies enjoy opportunities to claim credit for their supposed accomplishment. It matters little whether the firm would have located its plant in the same place even if the subsidies had not been offered (see Swanstrom, 1985; Feiock and Clingermayer, 1986; Stone and Sanders, 1987). This sort of policy making may hold little appeal for elected officials in reformed government, but in less reformed cities where politicians are more "accessible" to the public and where careerist motives are more likely, these policies may be quite attractive, especially in cities that are simultaneously undergoing fiscal stress (Sharp, 1991). The enactment and implementation of such measures, followed by subsequent ribbon-cutting ceremonies and public reports of factory openings, offer ambitious mayors and council members great opportunities to practice "the politics of announcement," in which credit is claimed for all that is bright and beautiful within the city (Stone and Sanders, 1987; Frieden and Sagalyn, 1989:281).

Political Skill, Formal Powers, and Development Policy Making

Reformed city governments may lack not only the incentive but also the power to pursue certain development efforts. Various small-scale projects and subsidies could be and sometimes are arranged by the city manager and other interested parties, but large projects involving multi-million dollar federal grants or commitments of substantial tax revenues, borrowing authority, or the government's sovereign power of eminent domain may be difficult for reformed governments to handle.

The successful implementation of development policy often requires executives to exercise internal control over city agencies and to deal effectively with external actors in the business community and in the state or federal government.

Political party resources as well as the formal powers of office are necessary for complex deals to be negotiated and carried out (see Pressman, 1972). As Barbara Ferman (1985) argues, a less fragmented political system provides greater opportunities for executive leadership. The challenge of internal control is especially relevant to the mayors of large cities.

> The ability of elected officials to achieve their preferred goals depends sub-
> stantially on their ability to control line departments, and frequently on their
> capacity to influence semi-independent authorities as well. The power to
> appoint and remove leaders of these agencies is an important route to con-
> trol, as is their capacity to reorganize and combine executive agencies. (Daniel-
> son and Doig, 1982:30).

Political institutions may shape political leadership and the ability of officials to deal effectively with external actors as well. The presence of unreformed political institutions such as partisan elections and strong mayor government provide the local executive the ability to "speak for the city" and act as an entrepreneur for economic development in deal-ing with private sector elites. For example, in his study of the strength-ening of the office of mayor in San Diego, Ed Sofen (1968) noted that important civic and business leaders frequently called upon the mayor to initiate policy. The mobilization of private interests in support of development projects is enhanced by a strong partisan mayor. As John Mollenkopf (1983:6) argues, successful pro-growth coalitions depend upon a political entrepreneur who gathers and risks political capital in support of development.

In the HUD *Economic Guidebook for Local Government* (1979), mayors are urged to take a leadership role in economic development because they must play a key role in marshalling the bureaucracy's resources, maneuvering public investment to attract private dollars, and manning the barricades when hard deals have to be struck:

> The mayor cannot abdicate the leadership role which is so crucial to a process
> as complicated as economic development. There are just too many players
> on the field for there not to be an active captain. (HUD, 1979:5).

Case studies illustrate the importance of a politically powerful mayor to economic development efforts. Mayor David Lawrence (Pittsburgh), Mayor Richard Daley (Chicago), Mayor George Lattimer (St. Paul), and Mayor William Donald Schaeffer (Baltimore) were the able counterparts of private sector leaders (Fosler and Berger, 1982).

The political resources of local officials also come into play when general public support or the support of specific groups in the commu-nity are necessary for the implementation of policies. Where strong polit-ical leadership is absent, the benefits of development policies may have to be fairly widely distributed if the necessary degree of public support is to be marshalled to implement the required policies and programs

(Hienstand, 1979). The salience of the institutional structure of local government and political leadership depends in large part on the type of development policies used by cities.

Development Policies

The policy instruments available to local government officials vary along a number of dimensions. Earlier work has attempted to clarify policies according to their visibility and the degree to which they are targeted (Feiock and Clingermayer, 1988). Policies also vary with regard to the amount of political skill and entrepreneurship by local executives that is necessary for their implementation. Five of the most popular local development instruments in the 1980s were tax abatement, industrial development bonds (IDBs), advertising, federal Urban Development Action Grants (UDAGs), and assistance centers for small businesses. The characteristics of each of these policies is examined in turn.

Tax Abatements

Tax abatements are a critical component of many cities' development efforts that epitomize the "deal-making" character of development policies. Abatements are negotiated on an individual basis with individual firms. Strong mayors typically play a critical role in negotiating tax abatements and in setting up the abatement district. Kevin White in Boston provides an example of how the ability of a mayor to control resources or influence those who control them leads to development success through tax abatement policies (Ferman, 1985:205).

Industrial Development Bonds

Although they cost the city very little in a direct way, IDBs provide a sizeable subsidy to private interests. Local government plays an active role in approving the bond and setting up the financing. Such policies are facilitated when a strong mayor with partisan support can deliver on the commitment to approve a bond issue.

Advertising

Advertising attempts to promote the community as allocation for investment. While seemingly simple, the internal management of advertising can be difficult because many interests in the community will likely want to shape the substance of advertising and promotion activities. Weak executives may yield to pressure to use promotion for internal boosterism rather than directing promotional activities to potential investors outside the community.

Urban Development Action Grants

The UDAG program explicitly emphasized cooperation between public officials and local business elites. UDAG grants were intended to leverage private investment for single projects that would not be undertaken in the absence of the support of the grants. UDAGs require public leadership and entrepreneurship in two respects. First, strong mayors seek out potential projects and solicit the support of private participants. Second, after gaining private sector commitments local leaders actively pursue federal funding for the projects. In this situation, the local executive acts as a lobbyist on behalf of new development vis-à-vis the federal government. Former New Orleans Mayor Ernest "Dutch" Morial provides an excellent example of how a strong mayor can use federal development grant programs. In 1980, 84.5 percent of the city's capital budget was from federal aid. Between June of 1978 and 1983, New Orleans received fifteen UDAG awards (Young, 1984).

Business Assistance

Business assistance involves policies to foster entrepreneurship and support small business ventures. This includes a variety of non-financial "ombudsman" type services (Premus, 1984). Political leadership is not critical to the success of these policies. Business assistance policies do not require specification or negotiation because they are available for all qualifying firms or individuals to take advantage of.

Data, Analysis, and Findings

In order to make a preliminary test of this institutionally focused explanation, we employed data collected from a nationwide mail survey of government officials responsible for economic development activities. Questionnaires were mailed to officials in each of the 397 municipalities in the United States with populations greater than 50,000, as of 1980. Of the 397 cities surveyed, 226 (57%) responded. The responses identified the development policies that were and were not used in the respondent cities between 1980 and 1985 (Feiock, 1985). The five development policies examined here were coded dichotomously as one, if in use during the study period, or as zero, if not in use.

The data analysis incorporates the argument focusing upon reformed institutions—described earlier—with two other sorts of alternative but not contradictory explanations. The first, perhaps best represented by the work of Rubin and Rubin (1987), contends that the use of economic development policies can best be explained by the presence of fiscal stress or economic need. Cities with the greatest need are expected to be the most likely to pursue development policies. We employ three different, frequently used indicators of city need: per capita personal income, city bond ratings, and population. The 1980 population in thousands (POPU-LATION) and per capita personal income for each city were taken from the U.S. Commerce Department's Census of Population. Ratings of the general obligation bonds for each municipality (BOND), as reported by Moody's Investor Services, were derived from the 1980 *Municipal Year-book*. Fiscally well-off cities with bond ratings of "Aaa" or "Aa" were coded as one, while cities with lower bond ratings were coded as zero.

Another kind of explanation examined in this analysis links the adoption of economic development policies to the activity of a pro-growth coalition of city elites and business interests, sometimes with support from media, civic organizations and labor unions. Active neighborhood organizations, according to this view, will be likely to deter development efforts. Examples of research in this vein include work by Molotch (1976), Friedland (1983), Fainstein, et al. (1983) and Schumaker, et al. (1986). This explanation is operationalized in this study using responses to four questions on the survey described above. The first question asked respondents was: "How active are civic and business organizations in the city?" (CIVIC). Responses of highly active were coded as one and responses of somewhat active or not active were coded as zero. The second indicator is taken from responses to the question, "Is there an over-arching or elite organization in the city which leads development efforts or coordinates the activities of other community groups?" (ELITE). This variable is coded as one if respondents indicated that such an organization was present and as zero if no such organization was said to be present. Thirdly, respondents were asked about the activity of neighborhood organizations (NEIGHBOR). Cities with active neighborhood organizations were coded as one while those with less active or inactive groups were coded as zero. Finally, development officials were asked how much the local media supported economic development efforts (MEDIA). Responses of high support were coded as one while responses of low or medium support were coded as zero.

Data on municipal institutional arrangements were derived from the International City Management Association's *Municipal Yearbook*. Cities with a mayor-council form of government were coded as one, while council-manager cities or cities with a commission form of government were coded as zero (MAYOR). Cities with some form of ward or district representation were coded as one, while cities with exclusively at-large representation were coded as zero (WARD). Cities with partisan elections were coded as one while non-partisan cities were coded as zero (PARTY). Finally, cities in which the mayor has a veto were coded as one while cities without a mayoral veto were coded as zero.

Each explanation treats the discrete choice of adoption of a policy as a function of some combination of the variables described above. Since the policy choices are dichotomous, we employed a logistical regression model to test these arguments.

The results of this analysis are presented in table 8.1. The results provide support for the hypotheses that political institutions in cities shape development choices. The table reports some support for each of the three explanations examined. Consistent with previous research, the adoption of development policy can be linked to economic conditions

Table 8.1   Logistic Regressions Predicting Development Policy Adoption

Independent Variable	UDAG	ADV	ASST	ABATE	IDB
CONSTANT	9.8867	7.9000	6.3368	4.9084	9.9431
POPULATION	.0022	.0001	.0006	.0001	.0001
	(9.45)	(3.45)	(6.36)	(3.13)	(2.47)
BOND	−.3593	−.3944	−.0794	.0531	−.2704
	(−6.91)	(−10.40)	(−2.50)	(1.47)	(−3.10)
INCOME	−.0012	−.0004	−.0001	−.0002	−.0001
	(−18.09)	(−17.28)	(−7.78)	(−8.65)	(−3.45)
CIVIC	.3770	.3761	.1714	.0617	−.0001
	(7.11)	(10.86)	(5.63)	(1.87)	(−1.42)
ELITE	.6326	−.0478	.1104	.3795	.7408
	(12.22)	(−1.35)	(3.57)	(10.66)	(4.65)
NEIGHBOR	−.3634	−.0219	−.1866	.2296	−.9962
	(−8.99)	(−0.88)	(−8.05)	(8.58)	(−4.65)
MEDIA	.2879	.0358	−.0288	−.0677	.7826
	(7.58)	(1.64)	(−3.49)	(−2.99)	(6.29)
MAYOR	.3350	.0169	.1718	.2434	.4979
	(4.78)	(0.28)	(3.42)	(5.59)	(3.35)
WARD	.4739	−.2276	.1181	.2554	2624
	(8.06)	(−7.16)	(3.58)	(6.95)	(2.17)
PARTY	.3183	.3154	.0507	.6697	.3062
	(14.37)	(7.53)	(−4.45)	(1.73)	(1.97)
VETO	.9682	.4318	−.2191	.0928	.2411
	(14.37)	(7.53)	(−4.45)	(1.73)	(1.97)
McKelvey r^2	.78	.34	.24	.28	.39
% predicted	93%	72%	69%	72%	93%

and the mobilization of development interests. For example, the need variables are consistently related to policy adoptions in the expected way. In addition, civic and elite group activity are positively related to the adoption of most development policies but neighborhood group activity is negatively related to UDAG projects, business assistance efforts, and the use of industrial development bonds. Media influence appears to influence UDAG and IDB adoptions significantly and positively.

After these forces are accounted for in the model, local political institutions have a significant effect on the adoption of specific development policy instruments. Institutions related to partisanship and mayoral leadership are strongly related to several development policies, particularly direct and visible initiatives such as UDAG projects. This suggests that institutional factors strengthening the executive may enhance the grantsmanship of city government. In addition, the analysis reveals that the mayor-council form of government is positively related to each of the five policy adoptions examined here. For four of the five policies, the relationship is statistically significant. The mayoral veto is very strongly associated with the use of UDAGs and advertising campaigns and also appears, though less strongly, to be related to the utilization of industrial development bonds and tax abatements. Perhaps these weaker effects upon IDBs and abatements reflect the routinization of these policy instruments as they become more pervasive (see Spindler and Forrester, 1991). Over time, these policies may be pursued in an increasingly standardized way, so the need for the mayor's political clout may be diminishing.

The results also reveal that ward representation is strongly and positively related to policies offering the prospect of geographically specific benefits, such as tax abatements, UDAGs, and IDBs. The only unexpected findings regarding these institutional variables were the negative relationships between ward representation and advertising, on the one hand, and mayor veto and business assistance centers, on the other. It may be that ward representation discourages advertising efforts because advertising offers little possibility for geographic targeting of benefits. The negative effect of mayor veto upon use of business assistance centers demonstrates that a strong executive is not needed to pursue this policy and that therefore cities with weak mayors may find them attractive alternatives to policies that appear to require more deal-making ability.

Discussion

These results have important implications for the practice of economic development in cities. Because certain types of policies require more visible leadership and entrepreneurship from local political officials, the characteristics of the political system may determine their likelihood of adoption. For example, projects like tax abatement which require negotiation between city hall and individual business representatives may be more feasible where the powers of local executives are substantial. Conversely, programs like business assistance may require more management skill than entrepreneurship and therefore be more successful in a reformed political environment.

Do not make too much of these findings that reveal a connection between institutional form and policy choice. It was never our intent to argue that institutional factors or institutionally focused explanations can account entirely for the adoption of economic development policies. Nor was it our claim that such an argument was superior to other arguments that focus upon need characteristics or growth conditions. Instead, our purpose was to demonstrate that institutions matter in very substantial ways in this policy area. The form of government that a city chooses (or has imposed upon it) does influence its ability to pursue certain kinds of policy options. This claim should come as no surprise to those who have actively sought to change local government arrangements. Most people have preferences over institutional arrangements not because those features are viewed as inherently good or evil but because they believe those characteristics of government lead to certain outcomes that are favored or disfavored. The institutional arrangements therefore are "second-order" choices that are determined by citizen support for "first-order" policy preferences.

For some citizens in some cities, preferences over municipal economic policy may dictate support for kinds of government and types of elected officials who are likely to pursue and achieve development ends that are popularly believed to promote job creation and fiscal health. Governmental forms and particular politicians who are unable or unwilling to master the art of the deal may fall into disfavor among those who favor official and deliberate economic development efforts by local government. This may ultimately lead to pressure for changes in local government. Some such changes have recently taken place within reformed governments, although the basis for this trend is still not clear. For example, council-manager cities today are more likely than not to have a directly elected mayor, much like conventional mayor-council governments (Protasel, 1988). Of course, not all citizens are interested in or supportive of development strategies, and in any case other policy questions may often be more salient. But for many cities, growth concerns and development policy instruments may be considered crucial. The traditional reformed city government may not long survive under those circumstances.

NINE

INDUSTRIAL DEVELOPMENT GROUPS, LOCAL DEPENDENCE, AND THE COMMUNITY GROWTH MACHINE

Craig R. Humphrey and Rodney A. Erickson

NONPROFIT LOCAL industrial development groups (LIDGs) are formally organized corporate or chartered associations of business leaders, political officials, and professionals who work to promote capital investment for manufacturing and other economic activities in American cities and towns.[1] While some LIDGs serve in a limited capacity as organizers and administrators of industrial revenue bond (IRB) programs, others are extremely active in a diverse and complex set of economic development efforts. Some LIDGs own and operate industrial parks and small incubators; others assist firms in taking advantage of state or local tax abatements, publicly subsidized low interest loan programs, and job training. Many advertise their home communities in newspapers, trade magazines, and other media.

As nonprofit entities, they share certain characteristics with the vast array of other institutions with the same status, ranging from philanthropic cultural foundations to social welfare organizations: (1) they cannot distribute surplus earnings to individual members; (2) they are exempt from federal taxation; and (3) they may receive tax-exempt gifts in the form of money, land, and other real property (Salamon, 1987:100). The legal corporate structure of the LIDGs suggests that their origins are state-approved. In fact, they actually are encouraged by state and federal tax policies and economic development programs throughout the United States, a characteristic which will take on considerable importance as this discussion unfolds.[2]

It is important to note that, while LIDGs have a long history in the United States, they substantially grew in numbers during the past two decades. This surge of growth is important to our discussion in at least two respects. First, the growth occurred when the United States was experiencing a massive industrial restructuring or deindustrialization with plant closings and disinvestment, capital reinvestment in manufacturing and other economic activities in new regions or other countries, and cutbacks in the size of the industrial labor force (Bluestone and Harrison, 1982; Piore and Sabel, 1984; Gottdiener, 1985). Deindustrialization has been especially pronounced in the old "Industrial Belt" of the American Midwest and Northeast.

The increase in the number of LIDGs in the United States also is significant because they have proliferated at a time when federal and state programs have been cut back dramatically. LIDGs began increasing in spite of this growing governmental conservatism, and they often involved the consolidation of fiscal resources in public-private partnerships (Fosler and Berger, 1982; Salamon and Abramson, 1986). Thus, increasingly scarce resources were being invested in efforts to create employment opportunities in the private sector at a time when job generation in the manufacturing sectors of most states and many localities was waning.

While there exists a large and somewhat controversial body of literature about many development tools and policies of LIDGs (such as their use of tax-exempt industrial revenue bonds), relatively little is known about their social organization, their networks of interaction, or their impact on the political, economic, and social life of their respective communities. Consequently, our discussion is organized around three central topics. First, we examine two closely related paradigms being developed by sociologists, geographers, and other social scientists to explain the rationale for the pervasive, ongoing, and highly organized economic development efforts in local communities across the United States. Second, we discuss the growing literature on LIDGs as one form of this social and geographical phenomenon. Surprisingly, the organization and impact of LIDGs are topics often overlooked in the sociological and geographical literature on local economic development. Finally, we turn to the significance of research on LIDGs for the literature and future research on local economic development.

Place Entrepreneurship and Local Dependence

At least two paradigms are currently being developed to explain the social basis and pervasiveness of local economic development efforts in advanced market economies such as the United States. Place entrepreneurship, otherwise known as the "growth machine" hypothesis, seeks to explain local development efforts in terms of a local rentier class or land-based elite struggling to enhance its class interests through increasing the demand and market value of land (Molotch, 1976a; Logan and Molotch, 1987). A second approach, the "local dependence" hypothesis, seeks to explain local development efforts in terms of the need for different classes, races, and/or ethnic groups that ordinarily have competing interests to collectively enhance the vitality of a local economy through unified efforts because of their dependence on (or commitment to) a particular geographic area or territory. The two hypotheses could be mutually exclusive in more conceptually developed forms, but neither one is sufficiently well developed to be considered anything other than an embryonic paradigm at present.

Place Entrepreneurship

Reproducing the class standing of the local rentier class or land-based elite requires place entrepreneurship to maximize the exchange value of their real property. Place entrepreneurs thus engage in collective action, often forming an alliance with public officials and others "to create the conditions that will intensify future land use in an area" (Logan and Molotch, 1987:32). Thus, the daily competitive behavior evident among local businesses in a community is constrained by a common interest in future prosperity, and this common denominator causes the intermittent surfacing of collective action to battle other places for capital investment, industry, and other sources of economic growth (Molotch, 1976a:311).

Rentiers' land-based interest in future prosperity does more than stimulate the formation of a well-organized development group harboring the expertise, energy, and financial resources of economic elites in a community. It also links these actors to public agencies and private trusts with the resources necessary to overcome whatever political and financial limitations a local growth machine might have (Feagin, 1985; 1988). Even Richard K. Mellon's Allegheny Conference on Community Development, formed in 1943, required the authority and finances of government to build a state park in downtown Pittsburgh, to control flooding for the espoused purpose of protecting land values in the central business district, and to increase the accessibility of this urban land through transportation improvements (Lubove, 1969; Alberts, 1981).[3]

As transportation and communications technologies reduce the importance of geographic site characteristics in determining the demand for and value of land (Wardwell, 1980; Castells, 1989), local growth policies and officially designated uses of land become more salient properties influencing which communities grow as well as the rate and nature of economic development (Gottdiener, 1977; Rudel, 1989). Consequently, places begin to engage in "fiscal zoning" whereby land use policies and capital improvement programs are designed to promote the activities most profitable to governmental bodies as well as private interests, including the rentiers (Logan, 1976a; 1976b; Molotch, 1976b). This approach may also help to explain the observed tendency for many municipalities to zone excessive amounts of land for industrial purposes, often far in excess of any reasonable expectations for this type of development (Erickson and Wollover, 1987). The net effect of these efforts for metropolitan areas or nonmetropolitan regions is a stratification of places. Thus, communities will become even more varied in their levels of public services, in the quality of these services, in per capita tax costs, and in the quality of the environment as determined by residential density, traffic congestion, and the availability of open space.

The combination of controlled industrial and/or commercial development becomes a particularly attractive strategy for fiscal zoning, since communities gain a large tax base without the costly public service demands created by the intensive residential subdivision of land (Molotch, 1976b; Logan and Golden, 1986). In growing regions where this strategy is most likely to develop, municipalities without the initial tax base to provide services for industrial plants, corporate headquarters, or research and development parks may be forced to engage in costly, public service-intensive, high density residential development. Thus, lower income groups, many of whom are service workers for these corporations, will be forced to live elsewhere, paying higher per capita taxes for the same or less adequate services in more congested environments.

No matter how much energy local rentiers invest in garnering public support for their endeavors through the promise of jobs and appeals to civic pride (Molotch, 1976), at least three trends emerging under conditions of advanced capitalism eventually can enervate their collective efforts. First, there is the trend toward capital concentration and the multi-locational firm (Gottdiener, 1985). Branch operations promote managers from within the organization, purchase necessary inputs from regional or national suppliers, and experience shutdowns and employment cutbacks more frequently than locally owned firms (Malmberg, 1990; Harrison and Bluestone, 1988). Second, new investments may be larger because of capital concentration. Larger residential subdivisions, commercial shopping centers, or other activities create higher demands for land, increase the costs of housing, and require more public services. These changes, in turn, usually result in higher property taxes and housing costs (Hartman, 1984; Trounstine and Christensen, 1982). Third, some forms of growth occurring in advanced market economies involve risky technology such as offshore oil drilling (Molotch, 1970), nuclear powered electricity generating stations (Walsh, 1988), or land previously contaminated by hazardous waste materials (Levine, 1982; Edelstein, 1988). Thus, the possibility of antigrowth movements to protect the use value of land increases (Molotch and Logan, 1984).

The Local Dependence Hypothesis

Geographers and other social scientists have also become interested in the pervasiveness of local economic development efforts in recent years. Some of these researchers have used the local dependence hypothesis rather than a rentier-based place entrepreneurship argument to explain the phenomenon of community growth promotion (Cox and Mair, 1988; Fleischmann and Feagin, 1987). While the local dependence hypothesis and place entrepreneurship are closely related, there are differences in the approaches. The local dependence hypothesis states that a select group of firms, public officials, and independent professionals such as lawyers and engineers depend upon the economic growth of an area for their livelihood. Thus, they become involved with community-based efforts to promote economic development, rather than class-based efforts identified by the growth machine hypothesis (Fitzgerald, 1991).

The class differences of capital and labor as well as the traditional separation of governmental powers and private interests break down under these circumstances, creating an opportunity for the formation of community-wide coalitions on the basis of perceived common interest. The result is one in which "divisions internal to the locality based on race, status, and class have been increasingly downplayed in favor of a unity embracing wide sections of the local population and its political representatives" (Cox and Mair, 1991:205). Communities thus become "agents" competing with other places for capital, jobs, and residents.[4] For this interclass coalition to form, business interests must co-opt government and labor leaders in a community, thereby gaining a wide variety of subsidies such as infrastructure grants, tax abatements, and wage concessions (Goodman, 1979; Harrison and Bluestone, 1988; Cox and Mair, 1991).

The dependence of private firms on local markets is not universal, however, so participation in local industrial development groups varies among the businesses in a given community. In the search for higher profits, some firms are able to adjust to changing production or market conditions easier than others. Large manufacturers, for example, can circumvent production or market constraints through the localization of branch plants in regions with nonunion labor or multiple sources of materials (Bluestone and Harrison, 1982). In like manner, retailers can form chain stores, automate their services, and hire low wage clerical and sales workers (Harrison, 1984). Lease of equipment and/or facilities is another means of limiting the extent of local dependence. But for many types of businesses—especially those with substantial fixed capital investments, unique regulatory requirements, or dependence upon goodwill established in a local market—either complete relocation, branching, or multi-sourcing may not be viable options. Public utilities, certain financial institutions, newspapers, and real estate firms are representatives of business firms in which it is particularly difficult, if not impossible, to operate anywhere but in a particular local community setting (Friedland, 1983; Fleischmann and Feagin, 1987).

Both private businesses and public officials confront their local dependence by forming downtown improvement associations, economic development committees, or revitalization organizations designed to maintain and enhance the flow of investment into the community (Green and Fleischmann, 1989). The attraction or retention of more capital and labor means that more links in a chain of local dependency will develop with increased demands for newspaper and television advertising, utility services, and real estate sales. The interaction between local industrial development groups and organizations such as the chamber of commerce and real estate boards or regional groups including utilities and regional planning associations reflects this local dependence (Humphrey, Erickson, and Ottensmeyer, 1989). While these intensified business and economic linkages also are recognized in the growth machine hypothesis, the basic catalysts for action in the dependence hypothesis are interclass interests, not a local rentier class and a few allies. When one such coalition engages in activities that imply a net loss of capital investment and employment in other communities, businesses, government, and other dependent groups in these places retaliate by engaging in equally competitive, community-based recruitment practices (Wolman, 1988).

It is evident that the local dependence hypothesis is distinctive because economic development efforts reflect more than the class interests of a local rentier class. Those groups involved with local development share "spatial immobility of some social relations, perhaps related to fixed investments in the built environment or to the particularization of social relations" (Cox and Mair, 1989:142). Thus, the many groups involved with local economic development efforts and recognized by writers using either the growth machine hypothesis or the local dependence hypothesis are incorporated into the analysis of local industrial development groups in a logical way. Determining precisely who is or is not dependent on a local economy remains problematic in this framework, although it is clear that large multilocational firms will not be central actors.

The growth machine hypothesis is distinctive in its recognition of class-based, intercommunity differences in local growth promotion strategies.

In suburbs, for example, we are beginning to see the emergence of unique strategies based upon the class structure of a place: exclusive, entirely residential suburbs; corporate industrial suburbs in the midst of relatively affluent, middle-class residential developments; and costly (in terms of public service provision), working-class, high-density residential areas. Even in large, economically and ethnically diverse central cities, intercommunity competition more often than not undermines the interests of labor (Fitzgerald, 1991:118). It is highly unlikely that industrial workers will gain as much from local industrial development efforts as small businesses, high-technology firms, or capital-intensive production enterprises. While the dependency hypothesis operates from the notion of interclass cooperation to enhance community welfare, the question of "Community as agent for whom?" remains a debatable one. Far more research needs to be done to specify the kinds of places engaging in particular forms of economic development and their distributional impacts.

The hypotheses of place entrepreneurship and local dependence converge on a number of important points. Both are based on a recognition of intensified intercommunity competition for capital and jobs in the wake of industrial restructuring in advanced capitalist economies. These hypotheses also recognize the importance of cooperative efforts between private and public interests. Municipal and state governments play especially important roles in promoting local industrial development efforts. As the two hypotheses stand, however, the outcomes of local economic development may or may not be the same in both interpretations. In the growth machine hypothesis, local industrial development efforts lead to local community conflict over the distributional effects of growth. In the local dependence hypothesis, it is unclear whether interclass cooperation leads to economic benefits for a diverse group of interests within the community or the protection of business interests through public subsidies. In addition, critics have charged that the local dependence hypothesis obscures the fundamental class, race, and ethnic bases of industrial development efforts by focusing on territorial organizations of presumably diverse class and other interest groups (Duncan and Savage, 1989; Gregson, 1987). It has been argued that the only way groups (such as labor), disadvantaged through industrial restructuring, can improve their lot is through interstate, intercommunity, class-based action such as the Tri-State Conference on Steel in the greater Pittsburgh metropolitan region (Fitzgerald, 1991).

Important differences between places in both the type of growth promotion selected or imposed upon a place by nearby competing places have been noted in the literature (Logan and Golden, 1986; Logan, 1976a); however, the social organization, activities, and impact of efforts as traditional as industrial development have only recently become the subject of much concerted empirical study. We now examine this emerging body of research on industrial development groups to gain further insight into the workings of local growth machines and the dependence hypothesis.

Local Industrial Development Groups

Although LIDGs have a long history in the United States dating back to the Depression and the efforts of state leaders in the South to make the transition from agriculture to manufacturing (Cobb, 1982), these groups have experienced a surge in growth throughout the nation during the past two decades. About 60 percent of all LIDGs chartered or recognized by state governments were formed in the decade between 1975 and 1985; thus, many are not much more than a decade old at most (Ottensmeyer, et al., 1987:574). Curiously enough, this trend represents somewhat of a sociological paradox. At a time when manufacturing employment is becoming a smaller and smaller part of the overall structure of opportunities for work in the United States,[5] a growing number of American communities are competing with one another for industrial jobs and investments, using the mechanisms of LIDGs in the process.

The LIDG Growth Phenomenon

One can gain some insight into this paradox by considering the resources devoted to LIDGs in most American communities. Simply stated, the financial and human resources invested in these agencies to some extent match the likelihood that their efforts will substantially alter the structure of local economies. Thus, one of the only national comparative analyses of LIDGs found that more than half of the groups studied spent less than $50,000 in 1984, and their total assets were less than $100,000 (Ottensmeyer, et al., 1987, p. 576). With these limited financial resources, it is not surprising that, in nearly 40 percent of the cases, LIDG staff size was limited to a single professional with clerical assistance and, in another 40 percent of the cases, LIDGs relied exclusively on volunteers.

Why have LIDGs been growing in prevalence throughout the United States, given their limited financial and human resources? For a number of decades going back as far as World War II, industrial managers have been relocating their more routinized production activities to other regions where labor and other costs were less expensive (Markusen, 1987:101-106; Bluestone and Harrison, 1982; Cox and Mair, 1991). This process accelerated for some manufacturing sectors in the late 1970s, undoubtedly triggered by the dramatic changes in energy costs after the OPEC oil embargo in 1973 and increasing global competition (U.S. Office of Technology Assessment, 1986). These processes of industrial change may help to explain why an estimated two-thirds of the LIDGs now are located in northern industrial states such as New York, Pennsylvania, Michigan, and Ohio (Humphrey, Erickson, and McCluskey, 1989:39; Green and Fleischmann, 1989).

When asked why LIDGs were formed, a national sample of their executive directors also provided insights into the recent growth of LIDGs. Almost 43 percent of them said that reducing unemployment was a key factor in the formation of their organization. Competing effectively with other places for economic development was the second most commonly cited reason for their formation. Taking advantage of state and federal programs for economic development was the third most important basis for the development of the LIDGs, according to the respondents (Humphrey, Erickson, and Ottensmeyer, 1989). Thus, both government and private local interests were influenced by the accelerated industrial restructuring of the 1970s and 1980s, and LIDGs were organizational manifestations of this influence.

It is also important to note that while the median staff and financial resources of LIDGs typically have been modest in the past, some LIDGs spend millions of dollars per year, employing large staffs directed by boards with as many as twenty-five community leaders from various sectors such as banking, retailing, and local government (Humphrey, Erickson, and Ottensmeyer, 1989:633). As industrial restructuring accelerated in the 1970s, some large LIDGs received national and international recognition for their expansive (and sometimes controversial) efforts to entice both foreign and American industrial investments into their communities. For example, in 1976, southwestern Pennsylvania's Pittsburgh-based Regional Industrial Development Corporation, working in concert with the Allegheny Conference on Community Development and the Commonwealth of Pennsylvania, successfully outbid other states for the location of an automotive assembly plant for Volkswagen, AG (Goodman, 1979; Westmoreland Community College, 1976).[6] As the national economic growth rate declined in the late 1970s, well-publicized examples such as this one encouraged both states and localities to initiate industrial development efforts, even if the odds of recovering the loss of industrial jobs were limited and the associated costs were high.[7]

While politically noteworthy cases may have helped popularize the cause of industrial development, especially in the changing Industrial Belt of the Midwest and Northeast, several other more subtle phenomena must also be considered to explain the growth of LIDGs under conditions of deindustrialization. Empirical work on the effectiveness of LIDGs in generating local employment from 1980 to 1984 estimated the financial costs of LIDGs' activities to have been very low. The median number of jobs created in a given year through the expansion of existing firms, new start-ups, and plant relocations was just over thirty, mostly in manufacturing. Given that the annual operating cost of an LIDG was less than $40,000 in 1983, the direct cost of creating jobs at that time was relatively low (Humphrey et al., 1988:11).[8] Some of this cost is also socialized, in that an estimated 40 percent of the LIDGs received at least a quarter of their annual budget from governmental sources (Ottensmeyer et al., 1987: 574). Hence, the public-private partnerships mentioned earlier serve to diffuse the risk of financing economic development efforts between those who can benefit through enhanced political legitimacy and others with a direct economic dependence on the growth of the local economy (O'Connor, 1973; Fleischmann and Feagin, 1987).

The legitimating efforts of public official support for LIDGs also played an important role in their recent growth. Private firms which depend upon the prosperity of local economies for their own survival often try to involve local public officials in the process of growth promotion (Rubin, 1986). The cutbacks in federal (and state) funding for various programs have put considerable pressure on local governments to find sources of revenue other than higher taxes, although they did take advantage of whatever state and federal funds that remained for economic development in the 1980s (Wolman, 1986). In addition, county and municipal governments are, by definition, the most locally dependent groups for two obvious reasons: (1) local government depends upon taxes to maintain and expand public services; and (2) local elected officials are held accountable for the health of their economies (Fainstein and Fainstein, 1989).

Social Networks

While the size and budget of the average LIDG are modest, this characteristic may understate the resources being invested in industrial development efforts throughout the United States. It is important to keep in mind that there has always been substantial variation across communities with respect to these efforts. In addition, analysis of the social networks of LIDGs and their extensive embeddedness in other institutions and agencies suggests that far more than the financial resources of LIDGs are invested in this form of local growth promotion.

The local networks of the groups include meetings, the exchange of information, and cooperative working arrangements with the chamber of commerce, boards of realtors, and manufacturing associations. Ties with the local chamber of commerce have been found to be especially extensive. LIDG directors hold regular meetings with chamber representatives, serve on committees, exchange information, work jointly to plan programs, and share personnel and facilities on occasion. Interaction with real estate boards and manufacturing associations has been less extensive, involving occasional meetings and the exchange of newsletters and other information (Humphrey, Erickson, and McCluskey, 1989:36).

LIDG directors and their boards also maintain an extensive set of periodic contacts with extralocal organizations, notably regional planning associations and public utilities. These contacts are especially important in that both groups commonly engage in their own economic development efforts on behalf of one or more LIDGs in a multicounty area. Between 20 and 30 percent of the LIDGs share work and have representation on the boards of these regional organizations.

Because LIDG directors and public officials are held accountable for the vitality of local economies, it is not surprising to find extensive interaction between the two groups. About 70 percent of the groups are in contact with local officials at least monthly, and frequent contacts with state officials also are common. This latter network reflects the various subsidized (often low-interest) loan programs, infrastructure projects, and economic development assistance often available from state government. Close budgetary connections between LIDGs and either municipal or county government also helps explain this network of relationships.

The social networks or connections of LIDGs are important in several respects. They create a conduit for the flow of resources, including financial support and information about prospective economic development interests of other local groups as well as potential opportunities inside and outside the community. The networking also represents an effort on the part of local groups to create conditions needed for the ongoing state economic development program (Cox and Mair, 1991). The prestige of board members and groups in the social network of LIDGs may have some bearing on the public and private financial support which the LIDG received. Research on other kinds of nonprofit groups places considerable emphasis on this consequence of social networks (Galakiewicz, 1985). Positive statistical relationships have been found between the extensiveness of LIDG networks, the size of the groups, their annual budgets, and even directors' estimates of their effectiveness in developing industry (Humphrey, Erickson, and McCluskey, 1989).

Directors' estimates of their effectiveness in expanding industrial employment, of course, represent only a part of the total gain and loss in local employment in a given period of time. Multivariate statistical analysis of total manufacturing and nonmanufacturing employment change in a national sample of LIDGs between 1977 and 1982 indicated that groups in nonmetropolitan communities, especially relatively large ones in growing states where wage rates were low, had a substantial advantage in garnering jobs and manufacturing firms during the period (Humphrey et al., 1988). In fact, some of the estimates of LIDG networks and connections correlated negatively with employment change during the period, suggesting that deindustrialization may have been an important reason for creating the social networks in the first place (Erickson et al., 1987:86).

The literature thus suggests that LIDGs may be cost effective in generating jobs within the limited confines of their resources. It also suggests that because of the political and social pressures being placed upon community leaders, especially political officials, LIDG activities occur in direct proportion to the degree of industrial restructuring occurring in a locality. The social and financial resources being invested in LIDG efforts may have some positive effect on economic development, as suggested by the responses of the LIDG directors to questions about their effectiveness. However, it would appear that these efforts, as vital as they may be in trying to protect the legitimacy and vitality of communities, at best retard the process of industrial restructuring.

Distributional Effects of LIDG Activities

Whether the increasingly prevalent activities of LIDGs represent public and private efforts to enhance the welfare of the community-at-large or the allocation of resources to a privileged elite is an issue which needs far more attention in this literature, particularly in light of potential differences between the growth machine and local dependence hypotheses. The leadership structure in these groups is biased toward banks, financial institutions, local retailers, and municipal government (Humphrey, Erickson, and McCluskey, 1989). Labor representatives rarely appear in the structure of leadership for these organizations, and civil rights groups or other equity forces only receive whatever indirect support they may have through municipal officials. Our own research found very little evidence of interclass cooperation in the structure of LIDG boards. As yet, little research has been published on the relationships between change in unemployment levels or income inequality and local expenditures for economic development.

Municipalities frequently establish industrial development groups wholly under the auspices of local government or, alternatively, charter public-private partnerships. Thus, the boundary between public and private interests is becoming obscured. In the case of public LIDGs, business and other private sector representatives often are asked to serve on advisory boards. Governmental officials are frequently represented among a majority of private sector members on the boards of local authorities or quasi-public corporations, sometimes chartered as nonprofit entities. In all of these instances public financial and other resources are being distributed to business interests, and there is a paucity of research on the distributional effects of these organizational structures and the policies they support (Humphrey, Erickson, and Ottensmeyer, 1989).

One empirical study of Illinois municipalities hypothesized that, in cities with economic restructuring problems and local leaders who accept the legitimacy of the public-private partnership approach to economic development, there would be an increase in the number of actions to promote industrial development as well as the likelihood that a coalition in some manner of LIDG would be formed (Rubin, 1986). A public-private partnership can provide a legitimate form for the amalgamation of public and private interests without the appearance that either is dominating the other. The forum also takes advantage of local public officials' lack of knowledge about the industrial development process and their need for private sector support, thereby reinforcing the prominence of pro-business attitudes. Such an arrangement provides both the necessary advice about development strategies, the opportunity to use public funds, and the appearance that decision making takes place outside of politics. Some LIDG executives even believe that a measure of success has been achieved when a development agenda has been formalized on paper (Humphrey, Erickson, and Ottensmeyer, 1989).

Rubin (1986) found considerable support for his hypothesis in Illinois municipalities. The presence of an economic development organization was strongly associated with a greater number of actions to promote economic development, irrespective of a place's location with respect to Chicago, metropolitan or nonmetropolitan status, tax rates, the level of poverty, unemployment, or past trends in population growth.

It has also been shown that more public financing of economic development, using infrastructure projects, low interest loans, and tax abatements, occurs in lower income communities. As the median income of places increases, economic development efforts may be financed through governmental programs or privately financed industrial revenue bond programs. Since lower income communities have high service demands and a relatively low tax base, they often are forced to charge residents more on a per capita basis (Logan, 1976a). Since lower income areas rely more on public funds for economic development, poorer communities are paying relatively more in scarce public revenue for economic development which may or may not benefit them in the foreseeable future (Rubin and Rubin, 1987).

Summary and Discussion

The study of LIDGs is instructive not only for providing insights into a growing form of local growth promotion in American cities and towns, but also for providing new ideas about the growth machine and the local dependence hypotheses. Given that at least 40 percent of the LIDGs in the United States receive at least one-fourth of their funding from public sources and that taking advantage of state and local programs for economic development is a major reason for their formation, the important role of government at several levels is obvious. State and local officials are an important part of the social network of LIDGs, and their socialization of the local industrial development process at a time when the United States, especially the Midwest and Northeast, is going through deindustrialization helps to explain the proliferation of LIDGs. Locally dependent groups such as retailers and financial institutions have very little to lose from the creation of these organizations, and municipal officials can present an image of attempting to cope with the restructuring of local industrial economies, even though the international forces at work to create this process are massive and overwhelming.

Ultimately, the rationale for forming or supporting a local economic development organization is based on the promise of jobs and additional capital investment. While our own research has uncovered evidence of positive relationships between LIDG budgets, the local and regional connections of the groups, and the number of jobs created, the net effect of these efforts amounts to retarding the deindustrialization process at little expense to private interests. Places with growing industrial economies are located in growing states with relatively low wage rates and large, but often nonmetropolitan, populations. Apparently, just the prospects for new employment may be a sufficient inducement for the participation of local officials and state government. Moreover, the infrastructure improvements often occurring in the industrial development process serve as ready inducements for local support, even by businesses not directly involved with an LIDG.

It is often argued in this literature that accelerated local economic development efforts and the public-private partnerships that often are a part of these efforts reflect declines in public funding for community growth. However, it should be pointed out that state and local public programs and the prospective funding derived from them appear to have been a very important reason for the surge in growth of LIDGs during the Reagan administration era. While local rentiers and others dependent upon the vitality of local economies provide powerful private sources of interest in this form of growth promotion, state and federal programs also play an important role. Curiously, we know little about the political and economic forces working at the state and federal level to create the fiscal climate necessary for local industrial development.

The literature on LIDGs provides considerable support for many dimensions of the frameworks being developed by sociologists and geographers. Control of the policy making and other activities of the

LIDG boards clearly rests with locally dependent business groups and their allies in government and certain professions. Representatives from banking, utilities, law, engineering, and related professions are at the heart of industrial development activities. Representatives from these elite groups form alliances with owners and managers of retail firms, regional utilities, planning associations, and local government.

Some groups characterized in the literature as central to local growth promotion, including realtors, land developers, manufacturers, and owners of local media, appear to be only marginally involved with industrial development efforts, primarily as part of their social network. This tendency may suggest that local growth machines have finer structures than the literature indicates, with a division of labor such that some groups promote industrial development while others pursue alternate means of protecting or enhancing the exchange value of land. Organized labor is almost systematically excluded from any direct role in this kind of growth coalition, although labor relations and wage rates are seen as central to an appropriate climate for effective growth promotion. One wonders if there may not be an inner circle of land-based elites in many communities that influences the efforts of these separate promotional efforts?

A strong convergence in local community politics emerges as places compete with one another in a territorially based struggle for industrial development (Humphrey, Erickson, and Ottensmeyer, 1989). Local dependence provides a useful framework for explaining the cooperation and/or capitulation of what might ordinarily be deemed competing community and class interests into a unified pursuit of local jobs and capital investment. However, the actual diversity of class interests in this effort may be overstated, particularly given the meager role of labor. Even though interclass cooperation may not be as pronounced as proponents of the dependency hypothesis suggest, LIDG activities have increased as communities compete with each other. Apparently, to do nothing is to concede defeat to the industrial restructuring process and to lose out to other, better-organized places (Humphrey, Erickson, and Ottensmeyer, 1989).

For state and local officials, industrial development organizations provide a source of legitimacy from their constituents and a springboard for action at a time when a growing number of voters have experienced economic hardship as a result of the industrial restructuring process. Consequently, industrial development groups become the conduits through which considerable subsidies for businesses and the communities flow and reinforce pro-business attitudes among local elected officials. These officials dare not oppose LIDG activities, for to do so would appear both antibusiness and anticommunity. Thus, the boundary between the public sector and the private sector is becoming more and more hazy (Humphrey, Erickson, and Ottensmeyer, 1989). Whether this effort provides social and economic benefits which go beyond subsidies to elite groups is a question meriting far more attention, since millions of American workers and their families have suffered immensely in the economic restructuring of industrial communities during the past several decades.

Another line of research meriting some attention in future work is the stratification of places and its consequences for local development strategies. In larger metropolitan communities, such as Boston, New York, or Philadelphia, there very well may be sets of specialized growth machines for industrial development, residential subdivision, the maintenance and expansion of public infrastructure, conventions and tourism, and others. The various groups may also be influenced by an upper class of banking, land, and utility interests. In nonmetropolitan regions, however, places may play unique regional roles as industrial centers, university communities, and residential communities differing sharply in their tax bases, service levels, and environmental quality. It is doubtful that smaller places in nonmetropolitan regions have the resources necessary for all of the conceivable growth promotion schemes, and some forms of development efforts are more compatible than others.

Characterizing the aggregate statistical characteristics and social organization of different places in relation to their ongoing growth promotion efforts, if in fact they are unique, would have some merit. Then students of local economic development could begin to think about different types of growth machines and dependent conditions, some of which may be creating more equity and stability for residents than others.

Notes

1. This chapter is based, in part, on research previously published by the authors (Humphrey, Erickson, and Ottensmeyer, 1989).
2. The legal and political history of these organizations in the United States is discussed by Salamon and Abramson (1986).
3. Similar examples of vital linkages between local growth machines and outside public agencies, such as the federal government and large corporations, are evident in Houston (Feagin, 1988), San Francisco (Hartman, 1984), and Atlanta (Stone, 1990).
4. This last point is one of several where the work of Cox and Mair (1988) and Logan and Molotch (1987) converge or diverge, depending upon the answer to the question, "Agent for whom?"
5. Hall (1987) notes that 4,219,700 jobs were created in the United States between 1980 and 1985. Of these jobs, only 33,200 were in manufacturing.

6. Incentives included over $90 million in the construction of a limited access road to the plant site, subsidized job training, tax holidays, and low interest loans from the Pennsylvania Industrial Development Authority. Volkswagen closed its Pennsylvania assembly plant in 1988, twelve years later. Part of the site now is being prepared for Japan's Sony Corporation.

7. Other recent examples include Honda's automobile assembly plant in Marysville, Ohio; General Motors' Saturn plant in Spring Hill, Tennessee; and Sematech Corporation, a government- and corporate-subsidized semiconductor research facility in Austin, Texas.

8. Inducements such as tax incentives or industrial revenue bonds are, of course, supported by public tax expenditures, and the below-market-value sale or lease of a LIDG's land or other physical assets clearly has associated opportunity costs. These hidden costs partly represent the extent to which local officials are willing to risk public funds to protect their own political legitimacy, so they are both economically and sociologically worthy of future research (Fleischmann and Feagin, 1987).

TEN

ASSESSING THE FEDERAL ROLE IN REVITALIZING YOUNGSTOWN, OHIO: LESSONS LEARNED OVER THE DECADE

Terry F. Buss and Roger J. Vaughan

YOUNGSTOWN IS a manufacturing city in the Mahoning Valley in eastern Ohio. Over the past decade, a wave of steel plant closings have wiped out three-quarters of its steel jobs and slashed manufacturing employment from 93,000 to below 50,000 today.

In response, state and local officials deployed the full arsenal of federal development programs including public works projects to generate short-term jobs, inducements for durable goods manufacturing firms to move into vacant land, subsidies for capital investment, worker retraining, and downtown revitalization. Despite the best of intentions and almost unlimited federal resources, they enjoyed little success. This chapter explores the reasons why federal development programs in Youngstown did not work and even delayed the implementation of more modest locally based programs that are now proving successful. Although our case study is of Youngstown, our work in numerous other communities and states suggests that the problems encountered and lessons learned are not unique. This evaluation, then, is intended to address a broad audience interested in understanding past development strategies or contemplating new ones in the future.

The Youngstown Experience

Within a few days of the first closing—in September 1977—community leaders proposed reopening the plants under community ownership supported by half a billion dollars in public subsidies and guaranteed public purchase of the output (Redburn and Buss, 1984). Neither this nor a more modest proposal to establish a steel technology center could attract the requisite private financing.

As an alternative, inducements were offered to durable goods manufacturers to offset the higher labor costs and other expenses that, leaders felt, inhibited growth. Despite using much bait, no fish were landed (Buss and Vaughan, 1987). The first nibble was ICX Aviation, which proposed a $150 million plant employing 4,000 people to build the YAK-40 commuter jet under license from the Soviet Union. The community spent $5 million preparing the facility, but the firm secured neither production rights nor private capital. To fill the gap, the U.S. Economic Development Administration (EDA) tried to attract the Commuter Aircraft Corporation (CAC). A $3.5 million Urban Development Action Grant (UDAG), together with loans advanced by a consortium of local banks guaranteed by federal, state, and local agencies, financed the reconfiguration of the ICX facility. But the project was finally foreclosed in 1983 because CAC, which had promised to employ 2,000 people, failed to find either private backers or customers. Subsequent negotiations with at least five other aviation companies were no more successful. The plant was eventually sold to a General Motors subsidiary at a bargain price.

Another rich package was offered to American Skyship, an American subsidiary of British Skyship proposing to build dirigibles for use by the Coast Guard and for private transportation. Despite free land at the municipal airport, a UDAG grant, and $10 million in industrial revenue bonds, no skyship was ever built.

Diversifying from aviation, the City of Youngstown announced that Kosmos Exports of West Germany would build a $30 million brewery employing 200 people. They were offered the largest UDAG ever awarded—$9.8 million—a state loan, revenue bonds, and free land. This project, too, spent public money but never broke ground.

Federal agencies funded other development efforts. Three industrial parks were built, but two remain nearly vacant, and the other is only one-third full. The city's main square was bricked over to create a plaza, but this diverted traffic so that local merchants have been forced to tear up parts of it. A regional post office has been built. Several historical buildings have been replaced with parking lots. And the mayor and local congressman have lobbied successfully for a new federal courthouse downtown—even though it would only consolidate federal employees from other office space now leased from the private sector. At this writing (April 1991), the courthouse has yet to be built, and prospects look slim.

The largest success so far has been the reopening of the McDonald Steel Works, closed by U.S. Steel and North Star Steel. A middle-level manager has reopened the McDonald works with private venture capital funds and has operated it profitably. North Star Steel is a subsidiary of the Cargill Corporation.

Why have public development programs achieved so little? An examination of development activities suggests five reasons—First, the priorities of those running federal programs may not be compatible with local development needs. Second, selecting projects solely because of their potential to create jobs leads to poor projects. Third, targeting programs at specific industries or firms often wastes resources. Fourth, subsidizing private capital investment, even if with federal funds, is expensive and frequently ineffective. And, those most harmed by economic problems are rarely helped by place-specific projects. In short, the guidelines adopted by all involved with Youngstown's development strategy led to a portfolio of projects and programs that yielded a low rate of return and much waste. These lessons are discussed, in turn, in the following sections.

Lesson 1: Federal Priorities May Not Be Compatible with Local Conditions

An economic crisis as severe as that faced in the Mahoning Valley puts state and local officials under enormous pressure from organized labor, businesses, and neighborhood coalitions, each demanding public subsidies, assistance, and compensation. State and local resources could not meet these demands. By relying on federal programs, local officials could help some people and refuse others, according to federal regulations, without feeling the political consequences. The cost seems deceptively small. But, over time, state and local development agencies unconsciously adopt federal priorities as their own and local agency staff become unable or uninterested in pursuing local opportunities.

Since the U.S. Department of Health and Human Services (HHS) requires that local welfare offices be centrally located for their clients' convenience, Youngstown planners relocated the offices in the basement of one of the remaining downtown department stores in 1980. Welfare clients could not afford to shop in the store, and their presence drove customers away, forcing the store to close—quickly followed by the closing of dozens of adjacent shops. Since the welfare department had a long-term lease, it remained.

When the DeBartolo Corporation, the nation's largest real estate developer, announced its intention to build a luxury hotel in a growing and wealthy suburb outside Youngstown's city limits, city officials nevertheless asked it to apply for a UDAG grant because they wanted credit for the project and the paybacks from the grant to finance other development activities. They felt that development programs needed a stream of "off-budget" federal monies. Washington refused the application. Nevertheless, the hotel was built.

Federal funds are not free and the adoption of federal priorities is not costless, although some of the costs are hidden. Youngstown does not need capital subsidies as strongly as it needs better education and training, streamlined permit-granting procedures, reduced bureaucracy, and better capital planning and budgeting (Vaughan and Buss, 1988). Yet, the focus on federal funds for capital projects meant that other needs were not addressed.

Overlooking Local Opportunity

Fixated on large-scale projects suitable for federal funding, Youngstown officials overlooked labor-saving or small projects. For example, Youngstown failed to capitalize on the growth of steel mini-mills. Ironically, a new mini-mill has been planned in Warren—a town twenty miles to the north—that will use, as feedstock, the dismembered parts of the obsolete furnaces and mills from Youngstown.

Officials also overlooked another steel-related new enterprise opportunity. Some of the departments in the shutdown mill sites, under proper management, could be made profitable again. A Fortune 500 company—L. B. Foster—leased a few buildings in Struthers, Ohio, the former Youngstown Sheet and Tube site, and has been making railroad spikes since 1982.

The Long-Term Cost of Poor Projects

The cost of poor projects is not simply that they do not work. They may require the investment of local funds later to bail them out or make corrections. Youngstown is rich in examples.

The bricking over of downtown streets is now being undone, but is being paid for by Community Development Block Grant and other Ohio Department of Development funds that could have been used elsewhere. To lease or sell space in a federally funded industrial park at an abandoned steel mill, local officials took any deal offered them without question. One tenant, Youngstown Steel, allegedly stripped and sold all of the scrap metal, raw materials, and building fixtures, and hundreds of thousands of dollars in equipment, which it did not own. When the company's EDA guaranteed loan of $10 million was exhausted, its officers left town. Much of the site has remained idle for five years because of court orders and litigation. Another tenant, whose business involved breaking down tires into carbon products, located in the park because the governing board was willing to waive storage regulations for its several million tires. The firm has gone out of business leaving mountains of unwanted tires and unleasable space.

Youngstown, responding to the philosophy of the federal Urban Renewal and Model Cities Program, demolished nearly one-half of its downtown. It then issued a general obligation bond to finance a municipal parking deck, which it leased, in a public/private partnership, to a local entrepreneur on terms that fail to leave the city enough to cover its debt-service payments, draining $553,000 a year from public coffers. The city has attempted to get the federal government to buy the deck (and the associated debt) as a site for its controversial courthouse.

Multiplication of Actors

Federal agencies have relationships with state and local governments, with local councils of governments, and with scores of economic development organizations. Many of the latter owe their entire existence and budgets to federal agencies, which absolves them from any need to "coordinate" or "cooperate" among themselves. The result is strong intraregional competition and the proliferation of plans.

The Mahoning Valley illustrates these problems clearly. The steel mill closings spawned numerous competing economic development corporations, task forces, and other groups. Before the closing, the only economic development entity in the region was the Regional Growth Division of the Youngstown Area Chamber of Commerce, which existed to promote the steel industry. This was quickly joined by the Western Reserve Economic Development Agency (WREDA), Eastgate Development and Transportation Agency (EDATA), Mahoning Valley Economic Development Corporation (MVEDC), CASTLO Community Improvement Corporation (CASTLO), Youngstown State University, Cushwa Center for Industrial Development, three Private Industry Councils (PICs) in a three-county area, Northern Ohio Valley Economic Development Agency (NOVEDA), Warren Redevelopment and Planning Agency (WRAP), Youngstown Revitalization Foundation (YRF), and a reconstituted Youngstown Area Chamber of Commerce acting as the Regional Growth Alliance (RGA). The state created its only satellite office of the Department of Development, which was intended to work with all these groups. In addition, each of four successive city administrations in Youngstown have appointed one or more task forces to deal with economic development. Displaced worker coalitions and neighborhood associations have also sprung up.

In summary, a community with a shrinking tax base and rising unemployment will be strongly tempted to use federal funds to revive its economy. Because they are free of state and local constitutional constraints, they can be used to subsidize private enterprise to stay in business or to start up in the community. Local officials are not held as accountable by local voters as tightly as they are over the expenditure of locally raised money (Buss and Redburn, 1987).

But the long-term costs of using federal funds may be high. Local opportunities may be overlooked in the desire to find projects that are eligible for federal support. Poor quality projects may incur unanticipated costs later that must be met from local revenues. And local government will become increasingly difficult to administer as more and more programs become dependent on federal agencies rather than on local elected officials for their budgets.

Lesson 2: Job Creation Is Only One Criterion among Many to Apply to Project Selection

Federal development officials—like their state and local counterparts—focus on jobs when funding projects. Jobs are the benefits that justify funding requests. Unfortunately, while the commitment to bring in jobs has powerful political appeal, job creation is a poor criterion to apply when selecting where to invest public funds. Jobs endure only if they produce something that people value. Trapped by their own development rhetoric, public officials rarely looked beyond the prospect of immediate jobs at the long-term prospects of the enterprises in which they were investing.

Short-Term Jobs

Youngstown's pursuit of a federal courthouse is an extreme example of chasing federal funds solely for short-term jobs. The region could have used its political leverage for other federally financed projects that offered more durable benefits. The finished courthouse will be of little value—with high commercial vacancy rates at 15 percent.

Although public projects may appear to create jobs, there are often state and local costs associated with federal funds that reduce employment elsewhere in the economy, because taxpayers must reduce their spending today to pay additional taxes or tomorrow to repay loans. Projects may still be worthwhile but must be judged by their long-term economic value, not by the short-term construction jobs they bring.

Indeed, given the efficiency loss incurred in the collection of tax dollars, there will probably be a net decline in jobs during construction of the project. It might be argued that the taxpayers' spending would have been on commodities purchased from out of state and that spending their money in state will create jobs. But a very large share of construction spending is for material that, for Youngstown, will have to be imported from the region, and construction labor is much more likely to be temporarily imported than labor in other industries because of its rigidly demarcated skills.

Multiplier Effects

Proponents of publicly funded projects often point out that they create additional jobs through a multiplier effect—as the paychecks of the construction workers (or, after the completion of the project, of the facility staff) circulate in the local economy. However, if there is an indirect effect of spending public dollars, there must also be an indirect effect of raising the money that more or less offsets the spending "multiplier." Analyzing the multiplier effect indicates where jobs are diverted by collecting taxes or borrowing and spending on the specific project. But these additional jobs are not a net benefit.

Convention centers are often promoted as the ideal economic development project. They create or retain construction jobs usually for a two or three year period while the center is constructed. They bring in outside dollars from conventioneers. And they spawn numerous ancillary businesses to support the center and its clients. Youngstown is pursuing such a venture based on the availability of state and federal funds. There is a catch, however. Feasibility studies have shown that few spin-off development activities will occur. More significantly, though, the center, if operating at capacity, would require an annual public subsidy of $700,000 to break even. This would not include interest charges and loan payments which would top a million dollars annually. Ironically, a local Holiday Inn recently constructed a private convention center just outside the city limits. It is failing and has been unable to pay property and other taxes owed the county. Yet Youngstown is still pursuing a public convention center.

Lesson 3: Development Programs Should Not Be Targeted

Communities pursuing federal funds must demonstrate that each project fits their overall development plan and that the project has a reasonable chance of success. This strengthens a natural predisposition toward the targeting of programs on certain industries.

The Mahoning Valley devoted much effort to little end chasing the aviation industry. Most state and local governments husband their small development budgets by identifying targets that have the greatest local development potential. The four most frequent targets are: (1) growth industries; (2) industries or firms whose output is sold outside the region or whose output is a substitute for goods imported into the region; (3) small businesses; and (4) high-technology firms. The reasons these targets are chosen reflect important truths about economic development. But the development process is too complex to use such simple rules.

Growth Industries

Most communities target industries that appear to have good prospects for growth either because the state's resources are compatible with the industry's demands or because the industry has strong growth prospects. In 1978, shortly after the closing of Youngstown Sheet and Tube, the Regional Economic Development Corporation, using EDA Comprehensive Economic Development Strategy (CEDS) funds, commissioned Battelle Laboratories to prepare a targeted industry strategy. Using "state-of-the-art" statistical techniques, Battelle identified dozens of industries as growth prospects. Now, ten years later, a review shows that in every case the growth industries precipitously declined and would have proved a poor investment for public or private funds.

In 1986, a private consulting firm was commissioned to conduct another target industry analysis. Two targets were gas and oil exploration and children's toys. Within a few weeks of the report's release, the petroleum industry took a nose dive virtually wiping out exploration in the region, and the only toy manufacturers declared bankruptcy. In 1991, Youngstown State University and the Chamber of Commerce conducted yet another targeted industry strategy, this time focusing on high technology firms.

Attractive as targeting is in theory, it rarely works in practice. Economic models cannot identify economic opportunities with any degree of precision: the models and data are too crude; and matching industries with local factor endowments is no indication of which industries will respond to public development programs. A cluster of target industries identified after manipulating economic statistics may be an appealing wish-list but should not guide the deployment of public development resources.

Published data on what determines business growth and location are weak. Even at the state level, data are available for relatively few of the hundreds of relevant factors that influence development and for few of the hundreds of different industries—accounting for less than half of employment and much less than half of net new jobs. Data at the local level are even more meager. And even where industry-wide data are available locally, they cannot be used to direct public subsidies or recruiters because production technologies or growth strategies vary so much among firms.

Even if growth industries could be identified, there is no way of identifying which industries might respond to public inducements or which inducements might be the most effective. There is no way of targeting a development strategy based on econometric analysis.

Export or Import Substituting Industries

Most federal development programs strongly favor industries that expand the export base of the local area—the employment and capital formation in firms serving markets outside the region. This policy reflects the plausible view that sectors serving local needs grow only if local income increases, which must be based on increased earnings of firms selling out of state (or producing goods that used to be imported). Firms selling in national markets will expand or contract less with the local economy.

But the distinction between firms that strengthen the local economic base and those that merely meet local demands is inappropriate to make in theory and impossible to make in practice. A successful new pizza restaurant serves it customers better pizza than its vanquished rivals and, if it is cheaper, allows them to spend their money on other things. More important, it may promote development indirectly. The successful pizza entrepreneur may expand into other businesses, use profits to finance other local enterprises, serve as a role model for other would-be local entrepreneurs, and train the local workforce. A pizza restaurant may appear a small boost to local development, but each dollar invested in it may stimulate more development than a dollar invested attracting tourists or building computers.

Despite the long held view that manufacturing employment is the export core of a local economy, in Cleveland, Ohio, the largest employer is the Cleveland Clinic, which employs 9,000 workers. The economy of Freeport, Maine, has boomed because of the expansion of a local retail store, L.L. Bean, which has been responsible for the successful growth of many local manufacturing firms by carrying their products.

The Youngstown area's largest employers are not export-based industries for the most part. The top ten employers in the city limits are non-manufacturing organizations, including: Western Reserve Care System, St. Elizabeth Hospital Medical Center, Youngstown Board of Education, Youngstown State University, City of Youngstown, Mahoning County, and the U.S. Postal Service.

Small Businesses

In a widely publicized economic development study, David Birch of MIT found that small businesses—those with fewer than twenty employees—were responsible for 80 percent of the new increase in employment between 1969 and 1976 (Birch, 1981). States have established numerous programs to assist small businesses, from technical assistance centers and loan programs to targeted procurement programs and one-stop regulatory agencies. Small businesses, however, are less important than new businesses in shaping state development. While many new businesses start small, development policy should emphasize the formation of new enterprises regardless of size and not small businesses regardless of age. Pay-offs from such a strategy can be great: in Arkansas, successful new businesses made up 36 percent of all firms in the state, and contributed 20 percent of the total jobs in the state.

Having been influenced by the importance of small business and the belief that a "capital gap" exists between lenders and small business, Youngstown created an interest write-down program. A review of the lending program for two years and $1 million shows that in nearly every case, existing, not new, businesses received funding. New ventures were not sought out and, in some cases, were shunned because they were perceived to be too risky.

High Technology

Shrinking employment among traditional industries has led some states to pursue high-tech firms as a source of employment for their manufacturing workforces. They are unlikely to succeed in this endeavor. The entire high-tech industry today accounts for 3 percent of the workforce and is anticipated to increase its share to no more than 4 percent by the end of the century. One new job in twenty-five will be in high-tech industries. Less than half of the jobs in high technology are well-paid and require advanced skills. The majority are unskilled production and clerical jobs that, as Atari has demonstrated, can easily move overseas.

Five states, California, Massachusetts, New York, New Jersey, and Texas, account for 60 percent of all high-tech jobs. Others are unlikely to be able to replicate the research infrastructure of these states—a necessary but not sufficient condition for concentrated high-tech development. States establishing an attractive entrepreneurial climate will stimulate the birth of new enterprises regardless of technology. Targeting high-tech will simply penalize those who are not in favored industries.

Seeing the success of other cities in spawning high-technology development, Youngstown decided to create its own program at Youngstown State University. The Ohio legislature allocated $10 million to YSU to set up a high-tech center that was to serve "as a regional resource." The center has state-of-the-art mainframe and microcomputers, robotics labs, and other exotic equipment. After two years of existence, the center is operating as a traditional academic computer center.

A second technology-oriented project was the funding of a small business incubator in October 1986, exclusively targeted toward high-tech firms. The incubator was funded under the State of Ohio's Thomas Alva Edison Program, local Job Training Partnership Act (JTPA) funds, and service fees charged to firms using Industrial Revenue Bonds. To date, only two high-tech entrepreneurs have come forward to participate.

Local development strategies have, with some prodding from federal agencies, targeted their efforts on certain types of firms. However, no way of operationally identifying targets has yet been developed. As a result, the portfolio of public development investments in Youngstown—in the form of low-interest rate loans, written-down land, and subsidized space—is not yielding a high rate of return.

Lesson 4: Development Programs Should Not Rely on Capital Subsidies

Because federally funded projects are discretionary and intended for projects that cannot be funded locally, communities use federal funds to offer large capital subsidies to foot-loose or branch firms. This is attractive to local elected officials who can establish their commitment to development at ground-breaking ceremonies, concentrate on a few politically active businesses, and offer a plausible economic reason for their actions.

There is, however, no guarantee that the subsidized firm is viable. In Youngstown, the promise of large subsidies and minimal risk to which private capital is exposed has made it almost impossible for federal and local agency staff to determine the long-run viability of firms applying for aid, because applicants have been unwilling to provide accurate information.

Nationwide, state, and local experience with capital subsidies shows that such subsidies are not an important determinant of private investment. In a survey reported in 1981, economist Michael Kieschnick reported that only half of all firms opening a new branch were even aware of the tax incentives offered by the state in which they were located (Vaughan, Pollard, and Dyer, 1984). In selecting a location, managers look not only at taxes and other financial subsidies but also at a host of other factors, including wages, labor force skills, unionization, energy cost and reliability, access to communications and transportation, the fiscal strength of state and local governments, and the quality of life. The little realized corollary is that companies that seek subsidies most assiduously—and Youngstown encountered many—may not be the strongest companies.

Sharon Steel is a major specialty steel company in western Pennsylvania, fifteen minutes from Youngstown. Although the company has asked for and received wage and benefit concessions from workers for several years, it continues to lose its market share. In 1987, the company received approval for a UDAG grant for modernization and expansion, but, before the ink on the grant had dried, the firm sought protection under Chapter XI of the bankruptcy laws. The UDAG was revoked, and the firm secured state and local aid. It is now once again nearing bankruptcy.

A local civil engineering firm in the region receives most of the contracts from the public sector for infrastructure design. It is highly profitable. The firm decided to build a new facility downtown to accommodate its growth. The firm received $300,000 under Youngstown's CDBG-financed interest write-down program as well as an industrial revenue bond. Undaunted, it lobbied for a healthy tax abatement, even though the firm could not move elsewhere without jeopardizing its future contracts with the city.

Subsidies to one firm destroy jobs and reduce economic activity elsewhere in the economy. For example, the Congressional Budget Office estimates that quotas on imported steel cost users of steel about $150,000 in higher prices for each job saved in the steel industry (see Vaughan, Pollard, and Dyer, 1984:35). The subsidy may cost more jobs indirectly than it preserves directly.

Lesson 5: It Is Difficult to Help Disadvantaged People by Targeting Programs at Disadvantaged Areas

All federal development programs embody strong incentives to help the economically disadvantaged (GAO, 1987). To be eligible for funds, in many cases, areas must demonstrate that they have above average incidence of poorly housed people, poverty, and unemployment. Proposals must show how the location and design of the project will create opportunities for the disadvantaged, and reports must document the extent to which these opportunities have been realized. But even poor people are mobile. Trying to help them by funding place-specific projects, such as downtown revitalization schemes or industrial parks, has been demonstrated to be a triumph of hope over experience.

In the late 1970s, the U.S. Department of Housing and Urban Development funded bricking over downtown Youngstown to create a mall to draw people back to retailers and create jobs for the poor concentrated in the urban center. Neither outcome was realized.

Youngstown's last department store closed in 1986. The city and state have given a private developer grants and loans to redevelop it as office space with ground floor retail space. But the offices will be occupied by computer/data processing experts from a local bank and white collar workers from a multistate pharmaceutical company, not the poor. The retailers will be boutiques, too expensive for the poor to afford.

A local developer donated land to a nonprofit corporation to create an industrial park several miles from the city, outside existing public transit routes. City, state, and federal funds paid for the necessary infrastructure improvements. The city justified its involvement because of the jobs created for the poor. However, the city did not institute hiring quotas to guarantee a percentage of jobs for its poor. This may be moot, since no public transit serves the area.

Epilogue: Youngstown Today

Although Youngstown's initial response to its economic crisis failed, some of the mistakes are now being corrected. Economic development programs are beginning to work, and some could even serve as a model for other communities. The major changes are due in large part to the dedicated efforts of community leaders, especially those from the private sector.

The greatest change is that the local chamber of commerce, after viewing the lack of progress in the region, reorganized itself to play a major role in economic development. Its programs were greatly expanded by attracting qualified professionals in management, business development, and marketing. The chamber has begun to address regional issues. Most importantly, it has established itself as the community "flagship" for economic development. It has effectively articulated the issues and implemented the philosophy embodied in this chapter.

ELEVEN

TRANSPORTATION AS A VARIABLE IN THE SITE SELECTION DECISIONS OF FIRMS: IMPLICATIONS FOR ECONOMIC DEVELOPMENT

William L. Waugh, Jr.

THE LITERATURE on state and local government economic development programs is replete with suggestions that transportation is a central consideration in the site selection decisions of firms. In large measure, the belief that transportation networks are crucial to economic development has guided federal and state highway building and river navigation programs and encouraged the development of rail networks, mass transit systems, and airports. Farm-to-city and city-to-city networks have been developed to facilitate economic interaction, as well. The issue to be addressed here is the extent to which transportation should be an important variable in current state and local government economic development programs. Data gathered in a national survey of firms will be used to gauge the importance of transportation variables in site selection decisions.

By all appearances, transportation is perceived to be a crucial pillar of economic development simply because it is one of the most frequent and most expensive components of state and local development programs. Indeed, the political debates seem to be most intense when focused on expenditures for such big ticket items as construction of highways, renovation and/or development of port facilities, expansion or construction of major airports, and other major capital projects to improve and expand transportation networks. At the same time, mass transit systems are competing frantically with highway-oriented state transportation departments for increasingly scarce federal dollars. States and communities are weighing the costs of building and maintaining transportation infrastructure against other critical needs, often foregoing maintenance in favor of more politically compelling needs. In that context, federal, state, and local governments are committing billions of dollars annually for transportation projects to attract new businesses, despite it being uncertain to what extent transportation spending encourages development.

Public Incentives for Business Relocation

It is certain that transportation is a popular development solution, however, and there are numerous reasons why transportation spending is popular in state and local government programs. First, it is still unclear just what factors firms value when making their site selection decisions and, thus, what incentives states and communities should be offering. The literature on economic development offers conflicting advice to state and local officials concerning where development dollars can be best spent. Good transportation networks, proximity to raw materials and customers, adequate and trained labor resources, venture capital, "hospitable" regulatory and tax environments, adequate and affordable energy resources, and potential for further expansion are all considered crucial factors in site selection decisions, according to both the common wisdom and the literature. But, there are indications that many of those factors are of only marginal importance to many firms.

For example, based on studies of business relocations in the Chicago area, Russell Smith (1985; 1986) argues that many firms, especially multi-establishment corporations, base siting decisions on criteria that are not closely tied to state and local development incentives. Smith concludes that such firms generally locate their top management offices in central cities with easy access to communication and financial networks, second level administrative offices in suburban locations that are less expensive and offer easy access, and production units in areas nearer to markets, labor supplies and transportation (1986:208). The production units may be much more vulnerable to corporate "divestment," that is, shutdown, employment contraction, or diversion of capital (1985:5) due to factors over which local governments have little or no control (1985:18), such as changes in the firm's market or internal financial factors. Smith recommends that local governments minimize large public investments in the relocations and, instead, concentrate on streamlining red tape, providing adequate and quality infrastructure and public services, facilitating the acquisition of facilities and land, targeting specific firms and/or industries, and "managing their dependency" on the new businesses to minimize the problems that might result from outmigration by firms (1985:12).

Industry and government studies have also concluded that taxes are not determining factors in the decisions made by manufacturing and other kinds of firms (Lynch, 1973:13–15; U.S. General Accounting Office, 1983:10). Experience with "free enterprise zones" has also borne out that conclusion (U.S. General Accounting Office, 1982; Welles, 1981), although not all agree that taxes are of so little importance (e.g., Rasmussen, Bendick, and Ledebur, 1982). With the interest in high-technology economic development in the 1980s, quality of life factors have been touted as a (if not *the*) major influence on business location decisions. Analysts and commentators have suggested that the decisions are influenced by everything from climate to cultural activities (Student, 1976; London, Crandall, and Seals, 1977), particularly when executive and technical personnel who will be moving to the new location participate in the selection (Waugh and Waugh, 1988a). It is understandable that transportation policymakers are focusing on the negative impact of traffic congestion or "gridlock" on the quality of life in many urban and suburban communities as an argument for more highway and mass transit spending.

Other studies have indicated that the criteria used in making site selection decisions may be quite complex, ranging from the "business climate" (meaning everything from local tax rates to how receptive the community is to new businesses) to the level of unionization and cost of labor to the aesthetic qualities of the location (Welles, 1981). In a recent study, considerable variation was found among the principal selection criteria used by "high tech" firms. Medium-sized firms (i.e., gross sales between $140 million and $800 million) indicated the greatest concern for the "intrinsic" factors or those having the most direct relationship to production, such as labor, taxes, raw materials, and transportation. All three categories of firms indicated that amenity factors were of low priority and labor quality and availability were of very high priority (Waugh and Waugh, 1988b). Those findings were consistent with a 1982 congressional study (U.S. Congress, Joint Economic Committee), but considerably different from the criteria suggested in a *Site Selection Handbook* study in 1983 (Conway Data), which suggested that "high tech" firms seek sites offering an intellectual base, a nucleus of scientific activity, good transportation (particularly airline) connections, aesthetic appeal, support for research laboratories, and campuslike industrial sites.

The criteria suggested by the *Site Selection Handbook* (Conway Data), in fact, are those that have guided a number of state economic development programs, such as that being implemented by the State of Kansas (Kansas Department of Economic Development, 1982; Waugh and Waugh, 1991). In essence, the criteria represent the Research Triangle and Silicon Valley development models. It has been suggested, too, that investments in transportation, most notably airport development, have been major contributions to the success of the Research Triangle, as have been investments in land use regulation, education, and other aspects of the infrastructure.

The Politics of Public Economic Inducements

Notwithstanding the confusion over the most effective inducements for business relocation, communities and states have implemented development programs concentrating alternately on such things as enterprise zones, free trade zones, industrial park development, job training programs, industrial revenue bonds, tax increment financing and other tax abatement schemes, quality education programs, and other presumed incentives for business relocation. Also, there are strong economic and political pressures to include development incentives, like transportation networks and tax incentives, that will also be advantageous to indigenous industries (Stone, 1984; Waugh and Waugh, 1988a and 1988b). Expenditures for highways, airports, rail and port facilities, and other transportation means may be of great benefit to indigenous businesses, whether they attract new businesses or not.

Second, the leveling effects of federal and state tax structures reduce the burden of state and local taxes through tax credits and other special financing and tax abatement programs. So, many economic incentives to choose particular locations are of minimal effect in the decision-making process, although reductions in federal transfers to state and local governments may increase the importance of tax climates (Shannon and McDowell, 1985). The firms may, in fact, relocate before they become property and income tax payers in the community (Smith, 1985). The industries, too, may pose considerable cost to the communities in terms of maintenance of infrastructure, provision of services, and damage to the environment. Communities that already have well-developed transportation networks can take advantage of current intergovernmental transfers supporting road and airport building and keeping rivers navigable to minimize extraordinary expenditures and to assure that the monies expended support infrastructure that will provide broad benefit to the community.

Third, the diffusion of economic development policies means attractive recruitment incentives will only provide a short-lived advantage; governments will have to concentrate on the incentives that take advantage of the most unique aspects of their communities. For many communities, particularly those located along major waterways or those that are airline hubs or highway junctures, transportation networks are distinctive assets. In short, those communities having the greatest potential for economic growth tend to be those with the best transportation links. Also, water access has been identified as a distinct advantage for urban areas interested in large-scale redevelopment projects (e.g., New York City's South Street Pier, Miami's Bayside, and Baltimore's Inner Harbor) and smaller communities seeking new service industries, such as the current interest among communities along the Mississippi River in legalized riverboat gambling as a stimulus for the development of tourism-related industries.

Fourth, unfocused and broad approaches to recruitment are much more expensive to maintain and harder to defend when budgets are tight and immediate results are demanded. Hence, there is a predisposition to fund economic development projects in those areas having the most potential for development—rather than those having the greatest need (Hansen, 1989). That has been a continuing problem in terms of targeting resources on poverty and unemployment in rural areas and small communities. "High-tech" development is attractive politically because it suggests "progress" and a "future-orientation" image in and of itself. The image belies reality, however. The capacity for high-tech development is not universal even at the state level (Kamienieki and Lackie, 1989) and the investment necessary to cultivate high-tech industry may be astronomical for some communities. In general, the incentives offered by state and local governments to lure "high-tech" firms have focused on programs to encourage research and technology transfer, human resource development, management training and assistance, venture capital, expansion of infrastructure and facilities, and recruitment and information gathering capacities (U.S. Congress, Office of Technology Assessment, 1984). Industrial parks are more popular than transportation networks, however.

An increasingly frequent focus of targeted economic development programs is small firms. They are attractive because they offer economic diversity to reduce the effects of recession, comparatively high employment potential, little strong competition with other local businesses, geographic dispersion, and spillover benefits to other businesses. Small firms, however, are more responsive to smaller economic investments than large firms (Waugh and Waugh, 1988a).

Fifth, communities are becoming more sensitive to the costs and benefits of specific kinds of industries. Development programs increasingly are seeking environmentally clean, proportionate (i.e., not too large for the available infrastructure), economically healthy, unobtrusive, and politically attractive industries that affirm the positive self-image of the community (Waugh and Waugh, 1988b). The kinds of industries that are labor intensive create large numbers of jobs, so prefer to locate near major transportation arteries. There is a danger, however, that businesses can put severe demands upon transportation networks that ultimately will prove expensive to host communities. Damage to roadways from large trucks, noise from rail yards and airports, air pollution caused by vehicle traffic, and other violence done to a community's quality of life are factors considered in recruiting new businesses.

Sixth, while there are strong indications that the major factors influencing many site selection decisions are beyond the reach of public policymakers, transportation programs are familiar and attractive. Improvement of the aesthetic qualities of a community, proximity to everything from natural resources to customers to educational institutions, availability of museums and art galleries, and so on may be either beyond the capacities of state and local governments (or any government for that matter) or too expensive to warrant serious consideration. Expanding or improving highways, ports, airports, and other transportation facilities produces benefits for existing as well as new businesses.

Seventh, the impetus behind many major recruitment drives is often a set of very specific economic problems endemic to that community or state and very specific economic goals to resolve those problems. Therefore, corporate recruitment, such as that incorporated into many "free enterprise zone" programs, has tended to focus increasingly on labor-intensive industries when unemployment is high, diverse industries when there is too much dependence on a few or on declining industries, manufacturing or service industries when appropriate for the available labor force, and so on. The effective corporate recruiters, in other words, are the states and communities that can provide just the right package of inducements to firms to tip the balance in favor of their sites, making best use of the unique factors in their communities and minimizing the expense of surplus incentives which have little or no impact on the decision to choose a particular site, while assuring that the industries thus selected are genuine assets to the communities in which they locate (Smith, 1985). While it is somewhat dangerous to generalize, manufacturing firms and other "low tech" and labor intensive businesses often are those dependent upon road and/or rail access to markets, customers, and raw materials. Labor-intensive service industries, too, often congregate near major transportation arteries.

Eighth, and last, state transportation departments were some of the very first participants in economic development programs and still tend to be influential political actors. Their influence, hence the influence of transportation policy, in economic development programs likely has increased during the fiscal crises in recent years. Funded by dedicated taxes, including earmarked federal funds, transportation departments have continued to mount large projects, particularly highway projects, when other departments have been forced to scale down.

In general, then, the question of how transportation policy can and should be tied to economic development is still unanswered, although the centrality of transportation to development is generally accepted. The task here is to examine the site selection criteria of businesses to determine the extent to which transportation is a concern and its importance relative to other selection criteria.

The Survey of Firms

Questionnaires were mailed to a sample of two hundred of the approximately eight hundred firms listed in *Business Week* as having high research and development expenditures relative to gross sales. The listing "R&D Scoreboard" is published annually and uses Standard and Poor's categorization of firm types. The listing was chosen because R&D expenditures are usually good indicators of the financial health of a firm, and it was expected to have a high percentage of firms in "expansion modes," that is, firms likely to consider expansions and relocations. The firms with high R&D expenditures may also be considered "high-technology" firms, according to the Office of Technology Assessment (U.S. Congress, 1984).

Firms classified as conglomerates and firms for which relocation would not be generally feasible, such as food and mining industries, were eliminated from the pool. A random sample was taken of the remaining firms. Mailings were conducted in 1984 and 1985. The sample size was reduced after the elimination of duplication when holding companies and subsidiaries were both sent questionnaires and with the elimination of firms that could not be contacted by mail. Ninety-three firms responded to the questionnaire. Twenty-eight indicated that company policy and/or concerns about the sensitivity of information precluded participation, and sixty-five answered some or all of the questions asked. With the aforementioned adjustments, the response rate was approximately 50 percent.

Due to the large number of Standard and Poor's categories (thirty-two) the firms were divided into four groups: information processing and telecommunications; heavy manufacturing; higher technology or light manufacturing; and primary industry. The information processing group included firms producing computers, peripherals, software and information services, instruments (measuring devices, controls, etc.), semiconductors, and telecommunications services. The heavy manufacturing group included those firms classified as aerospace, appliance, automotive, electrical, leisure time industries, farm and construction machinery, machine tools and industrial and mining machinery, and miscellaneous manufacturing. The high technology and light industry group included firms producing drugs, electronics, and office equipment.

Finally, the group of "primary industry" firms included a variety of firm types that did not fit into the first three categories, such as building materials, chemicals, fuel, metals and mining, paper, and textiles. The last category included most of the firms in the survey that were judged to be restricted to certain kinds of locales and basic industries more closely tied to their sources of raw materials.

The Expectations

While the literature on economic development strongly suggests that there are site selection criteria that are firm- or industry-specific, there are few prescriptions for developing recruitment strategies for particular firms. The expectation in the survey was that the more "high-technology" firms would conform to the patterns suggested in the literature as well as to general perceptions. That is, it was expected that the information processing and telecommunications firms would be more responsive to incentive programs featuring quality-of-life factors and university-industry information transfers and cross-fertilization, as well as to some of the more traditional factors such as the availability and skill levels of the workforce. The information processing and telecommunications group was expected to be largely unconcerned about raw materials, proximity to markets, and other "production-oriented" variables, like transportation.

The heavy manufacturing group was expected to be much more oriented toward the traditional concerns of labor, state and local regulations, taxes, raw materials, energy costs, transportation, markets, and customers than the first group. Given the relatively high levels of unionization in heavy industry and the relatively lower skill levels required, the expectation was that labor costs would be more important to those firms than labor availability and skills. Heavy industries were expected to be much less interested in the amenity factors as well. Transportation-related factors, in other words, were expected to be major concerns among the heavy manufacturing firms.

By contrast, the expectation was that higher technology, light manufacturing firms would be a little less interested in transportation and the traditional production concerns and slightly more interested in the amenity factors and information transfers than the heavy industries.

The expectations concerning the last category of firms, "primary industries," were mixed. By and large, the expectations were that those firms would be less technologically oriented, less interested in transfers of information and amenity factors, and more interested in transportation, state and local regulations, and the traditional production variables. Given the nature of their production processes and their products, transportation concerns would be a logical priority.

Data Analysis

Most of the firms were large, often with several hundred plants and offices. In terms of the general responses to questions concerning relocation experience and interest, 78 percent indicated that their markets had expanded during the previous five years. Eighty-nine percent of the firms indicated that they had relocated some or all of their facilities in the previous two years. Sixty-one percent of the firms indicated that they planned to relocate some of their facilities in the following two years. The expectation that the firms would likely be in "expansion modes" was borne out.

How important the firms viewed specific site selection criteria is indicated in table 11.1. While there is a great deal of similarity in how the four types of firms ranked the criteria, there are also important differences. Relative to the expectations noted earlier, the data substantiate some and certainly fail to do so for others.

Among the information processing firms, that is, the more high-tech firms, transportation was clearly not a major concern. Transportation facilities ranked only tenth on their list of priorities. Other transportation-related criteria also ranked very low, with access to markets ranking twelfth, proximity to customers ranking thirteenth, and access (a function of distance as well as availability) to raw materials ranking fourteenth.

Among the heavy manufacturing firms, transportation facilities ranked sixth as a priority. Access of markets, access to raw materials, and proximity to customers ranked only eleventh, twelfth, and thirteenth (respectively).

The responses of businesspersons from the light manufacturing firms were similar to those from the heavy manufacturing firms. Transportation facilities ranked sixth, access to markets ranked tenth, access to raw materials ranked twelfth, and proximity to customers ranked fourteenth.

Transportation was a more evident concern among businesspersons from so-called "primary industries." They ranked transportation facilities third on their list of priorities, and access to markets first, proximity to customers second, and access to raw materials sixth.

In general terms, if we can accept that information processing firms are the "highest tech" group followed by light manufacturing, heavy manufacturing, and primary industry firms, the data would suggest that the higher the level of a firm's technology, the less important the transportation-related variables are in site selection decisions. Also, the more labor intensive the mode of production, the more important the transportation variables. Beyond that it is difficult to generalize. Labor-related variables were given a higher priority by the more technologically sophisticated firms. As expected, the availability of skilled labor was high, ranking first, on the lists of the information processing and light manufacturing firms. Labor costs were also high on the lists of the heavy and light manufacturing groups.

Table 11.1   Site Selection Criteria as Prioritized by Firm-Type

Information Processing Firms (Rank)	Heavy Manufacturing Firms (Rank)	Light Manufacturing Firms (Rank)	Primary Industry Firms (Rank)
1. Labor skills	Labor costs	Labor skills	Access to markets
2. Potential for expansion	State/local regulation	Labor costs	Proximity to customers
3. Business atmosphere	Tax climate	State/local regulation	Transportation facilities
4. State/local regulation	Energy costs and availability	Tax climate	State/local regulation
5. Cost – land & construction	Labor skills	Potential for expansion	Energy costs
6. Labor costs	Transportation facilities	Transportation facilities	Access to raw materials
7. Tax climate	Business atmosphere	Business atmosphere	Tax climate
8. Social climate	Potential for expansion	Cost – land & construction	Potential for expansion
9. Proximity to university	Cost of living	Energy costs	Labor skills
10. Transportation facilities	Social climate	Access to markets	Cost – land & construction
11. Cost of living	Access to markets	Cost of living	Labor costs
12. Access to markets	Access to raw materials	Access to raw materials	Business atmosphere
13. Proximity to customers	Proximity to customers	Social climate	Social climate
14. Access to raw materials	Cost – land & construction	Proximity to customers	Cost of living
15. Recreation facilities	Cultural amenities	Proximity to university	Cultural amenities
16. Climate	Recreation facilities	Cultural amenities	Recreation facilities
17. Energy costs/availability	Proximity to university	Recreation facilities	Climate
18. Cultural amenities	Climate	Climate	Proximity to university

Adapted from Waugh and Waugh (1988b).

As a point of interest, in terms of the quality of life or amenity factors, none of the groups expressed a strong interest, although the information processing group response was slightly more positive. Tax climate was ranked a bit higher on all four listings than the literature might suggest. The community social climate and cost of living concerns were in the middle range in most of the rankings. Recreation facilities, climate of the region, and cultural amenities were low on all the lists.

Implications for Economic Development Programs

What do the data mean for transportation policy as a component of state and local economic development programs? For information processing, telecommunications, and semiconductor firms, the most important considerations are clearly the skills and availability of labor. Other factors may enter into the site selection equation and may tip the balance in favor of a particular location, but labor is the primary concern. Expenditures on transportation facilities are not suggested.

For heavy manufacturing firms, the crucial variables are labor costs, tax climate, regulatory practices, and energy costs and availability. Tax incentives and regulatory relief are more crucial to economic development programs than are transportation-related factors.

Like the information processing firms, light manufacturing firms appear to put greatest emphasis on labor, followed by regulatory practices and tax climates. Training and education programs, as well as tax incentives and regulatory reforms, are the best "bait" to recruit such firms. Here, too, transportation is not a high priority.

The last category, the "primary industries," would appear to be much less influenced by factors amenable to government manipulation, with the exception of a strong interest in transportation facilities. Affecting access to customers and markets and energy costs are beyond the means of most communities, but good highway networks and other transportation-related incentives might move a firm short distances.

The data are also notable for what they do not show. A high priority for access to air transportation is assumed in many analyses of economic development incentives. The comparative advantage presumed for communities with frequent and extensive air connections with major cities was not addressed by the survey. The respondents from firms of all types indicated strong desires to locate in urban or suburban areas. Roughly 5 percent indicated a willingness to locate in rural areas, but it was clear that proximity to urban areas with relatively well-developed transportation and communication networks, as well as cultural and social amenities, was a preference. Indeed, given the nature of the study and the sensitivity of the business community to the need to appear "business-like," it is likely that the importance of amenity factors was understated. If that is in fact the case, transportation may be less a priority among some of the firms than the data would suggest.

Based on the literature and the survey, transportation variables would seem to have only a marginal impact on the site selection decisions of firms, with that impact tied closely to the obvious needs for transporting raw materials to processing facilities and finished goods to markets. To some extent, transportation concerns manifest themselves as preferences for urban or suburban locations for facilities. Labor availability and skills have much greater impact on the site selection decisions of firms. As Russell Smith noted (1985 and 1986), the best strategy may be to think of infrastructure investment as long-term capacity-building for a community, necessarily proportionate to expected community needs, and not attempt to make large investments of public monies to recruit specific firms. Transportation investment alone will not be sufficient reason for a firm to pick a particular site, although a lack of adequate investment in such infrastructure and its maintenance may well dissuade relocation.

TWELVE

ORGANIZATIONAL IMPACTS ON FIRM LOCATION DECISIONS: THE EFFECTS OF AGE, SIZE, TECHNOLOGY, AND INDUSTRY[1]

Douglas A. Henderson, Stuart L. Hart, and Daniel R. Denison

IN ATTEMPTING to attract and retain firms in their own regions, state and local governments often try to provide a set of incentives that will match the preferences of individual firms. Planners may, for example, court high-tech firms with an analysis of the local labor force, manufacturing firms with tax abatements, or large corporations with descriptions of the overall quality of life of the region. Each of these strategies presumes that *different types of firms* will respond positively to different sets of location factors (Beaumont and Hovey, 1985).

Traditional industrial location theory, however, has made few distinctions regarding the behavior of different types of firms. From the traditional perspective, location decisions are presumed to be driven by "least cost" criteria emphasizing factors such as utility and transportation costs, state and local taxes, and labor costs (Hoover, 1948; Chapman and Walker, 1987; Blair and Premus, 1987). Often characterized as "smoke stack chasing," this form of economic development has usually focused on large, mature firms in manufacturing industries. In contrast, more recent trends in industrial location theory, particularly as it applies to high-technology firms, have emphasized a different set of criteria, often described as "ambiance" or overall "quality of life" (Malecki, 1984, 1985; Galbraith, 1985; Jarboe, 1986; Malecki, 1987; Denison and Hart, 1987). This approach concentrates on a different set of factors, such as environmental quality, proximity to residence, or cultural and recreational opportunities, and has often been linked to the location decisions of new technology based firms (Wiewel, deBettencourt, and Mier, 1982; Twaites and Oakey, 1985).

Since the early studies that formed the basis for least-cost industrial location theory were limited by their exclusive focus on large manufacturing firms, and the more recent studies that have identified quality of life criteria are largely based on studies of high-technology firms, there are few bases for comparison of the location preferences of different types of firms. In part, this is because studies that consider differences among firms have been few and far between in industrial location research. For example, few research studies have compared location preferences across industrial sectors despite the obvious significance for economic development. Even fewer have attempted to compare and contrast the locational preferences of firms at different levels of technological sophistication (i.e., "low" versus "high" technology). Combined with the relatively few studies that analyze location preferences by age and size, this lack of research may help explain a contemporary paradox: economic development planners seem to be offering incentives that most recent empirical research suggests have little or no influence (Wolman, 1988). Hence, if the traditional industrial location theories do not reflect the needs of emerging industries, the criteria used by many economic development planners may be inaccurate, outdated, and inappropriate for long-range planning and policy-making.

The question addressed by this chapter is a simple one: how do organizational differences influence a firm's preferences regarding location? For example, do large firms have different locational criteria than small firms? Do new firms value different locational criteria than older firms? Do low-technology firms really respond to tax incentives more than high-technology firms? The practical relevance of these questions stems from the increasing effort expended by public managers on providing industrial location incentives: if different size firms of different levels of technological sophistication indicate the same preferences, then it makes little sense to target incentives based on size or on technology.

Drawing upon the responses of CEOs from Michigan's "Automation Alley," this chapter summarizes a five-year investigation into the organizational influences on location preferences as developed in one book (Denison and Hart, 1987) and several articles (Hart and Denison, 1987; Hart, Denison, and Henderson, 1989; Hart, Henderson, and Denison, 1989). In all of these, the goal was to identify leverage points in attracting—or perhaps avoiding—certain firms based on their location preferences. In addition to reviewing differences in location preferences by age and size, this chapter also reports the results of locational preferences of firms across different industrial sectors and various levels of technological sophistication. First, however, is a review of the location preference literature. The objective is not only to develop a contingency framework for understanding industrial location preferences that better reflect the contemporary economy, but also to fashion an approach useful for development planners in reaching the goal of attracting and developing industry in their area.

Determinants of Firm Location

The reasons why firms locate where they do has been a topic of investigation for more than six decades (Chapman and Walker, 1987; Blair and Premus, 1987). At issue is the degree of influence various factors have in the location decision process. Considering research from economic geography, regional economics, and economic development, two extremes dominate the literature: (1) a least-cost perspective; and (2) an area infrastructure and "ambiance" point of view.

Least-Cost Factors

Classical location theory suggests that firms choose a location that minimizes their costs, either real or perceived. As a consequence, it should be reasonable to expect low margin-to-weight manufacturers to locate closer to resources and markets (Hoover, 1948). The "friction of distance" variables, as these factors are known, measure the costs of moving materials, products, people, or ideas across space, measured in miles, money, or time. For heavy manufacturing such factors would be expected to dominate location decisions, while noneconomic factors would be of little importance.

Recently, Wolman (1988) showed that empirical evidence supporting a least-cost view of industrial location is far from established, however. Chapman and Walker (1987), Blair and Premus (1987), and Bozeman and Bozeman (1987) have made similar observations. Wasylenko (1980) and Due (1961) suggested that taxes play an insignificant role in a firm's choice of location. Carlton, in a regression analysis, found that tax variables often were of the wrong sign, usually very small, and almost always statistically insignificant (1983:447). Fox (1981), on the other hand, concluded that property tax and other fiscal variables had a negative impact on business location. Newman and Sullivan (1988), Charney (1983), and McGuire (1985) also suggested that least-cost measures such as tax differentials and incentives schemes affect location decisions negatively. Bartik (1984) marshalled evidence that union sympathies of states had a major effect on business location and that state taxes affect business location, although the tax effects were of modest magnitude. Grieson et al. (1977) found manufacturing firms were severely affected by taxes in their location decision while nonmanufacturing firms were not. Bartik (1988) found no effect of environmental regulations on business location decisions.

Mandell (1972) showed that proximity to customers was the greatest locational advantage for manufacturing firms in the Detroit, Michigan, area. Distance to suppliers was also significant for manufacturers choosing plant locations in the area, as were state and local business taxes (Mandell 1972:4). Disadvantages of Detroit as an industrial location included low labor productivity and relatively high business taxes. In addition, Tybout and Mattila (1977:12) found that average property taxes had a significant effect on the business location decisions of Detroit manufacturing firms.

Area Infrastructure

A second set of location criteria are concerned not with proximity but with the characteristics or attributes of a given area (Rees, 1986; Premus, 1982; McLoughlin, 1983). Included here are economic variables such as labor availability and organization, physical issues such as infrastructure, power, and water, and less concrete issues such as quality of life (QOL) (Harding 1988). A good deal of evidence gathered over the last fifteen years from several regions of the United States suggests that least-cost locational criteria may now have given way to QOL considerations in industrial location preferences (Hart and Denison, 1987; Blair and Premus, 1987; Jarboe, 1986; Galbraith, 1985). Indeed, as the human skill factor has become a more important variable in the past two decades and as telecommunications have improved, distance to suppliers/markets and state and local taxes have become less critical in choosing new industrial locations (Lyne, 1988). A plant started in a community that ranks low on the "livability scale" will soon have difficulty in attracting, or even transferring, engineers and managers, according to Rees (1986). Similarly, access to a good airport has become more valuable for such firms than either access to raw materials or proximity to large population centers (O'Conner, 1987).

Several researchers reach similar conclusions on the amenity influence (Roberts, 1970; Premus, 1982; Gorlow, 1984; Hicks, 1985; Blair and Premus, 1987; de Noble and Galbraith, 1987; Watts, 1987). However, the vast majority of these studies have focused on the East and West Coasts of the United States—Route 128, Silicon Valley or Orange County, California, in particular—with other parts of the nation or world given little coverage. For example, Roberts (1970) and Cooper and Bruno (1977) established that the locational preferences of high-technology firms in the Route 128 area around Boston, Massachusetts, and Silicon Valley used criteria other than the traditional least-cost factors in making location decisions.

More recently, Galbraith (1985) and de Noble and Galbraith (1987) surveyed high-technology firms in Orange County and San Diego County, California, concerning their location criteria. The authors concluded the most important locational component for high-technology firms in these locations was "ambiance." Jarboe's (1986) results for forty-six high-technology firms in the Ann Arbor, Michigan, area indicated that the key locational strengths of the area were its universities, QOL, airport access, and workforce. For this study, firms were generally small, rapidly growing, new companies with a large percentage of their personnel devoted to research and development activities. It should be kept in mind that such QOL conclusions are based exclusively on studies of high-technology businesses, with little consideration given to the range of economic activities local governments usually spend time trying to attract and develop — manufacturing, wholesale, retail, and service industries.

None of the above studies, however, whether addressing least-cost or infrastructure factors, explains the current paradox in economic development — why political actors continue to offer tax differentials and fiscal incentives even though the empirical literature shows these to be of little influence in the actual firm location decision process (Wolman, 1988). Wolman suggests two explanations for the paradox: (1) the "conventional wisdom" derived from research findings is either wrong or has been misinterpreted; or (2) offering least-cost incentives makes good sense politically for those charged with the responsibility for economic development. A third explanation can be offered — that previous research has not gone far enough.

Organizational Contingencies in Location Decisions

Considering the specificity that local economic development managers need, most past research efforts suffer from a lack of attention given to the specific organizational and strategic characteristics of the "firm." Few studies have explicitly linked location preferences to characteristics of the firm, but two studies have offered some empirical evidence in this direction. First, McDermott and Taylor (1976) investigated the locational preferences of New Zealand manufacturing firms with respect to five considerations of organizational form: (1) age, (2) management type, (3) plant status, (4) location, and (5) employment size. No striking statistical variations were evident, but managers did discriminate among some individual elements of their local environment, especially in relation to the location, management characteristics, age, and size of their firms (McDermott and Taylor, 1976:332). Unfortunately, because McDermott and Taylor's (1976) study occurred when technology was not a driving force in regional economic development and parts of their design — the firm size brackets, in particular — were unclearly identified, it is difficult to capture the relative magnitude of the differences these variables carry with them in today's business environment.

Second, Malizia (1984), through a survey of 136 manufacturing firms in North Carolina, South Carolina, and Virginia, investigated locational preferences in relation to several organizational characteristics: (1) location (North Carolina, South Carolina, or Virginia); (2) type of firm (independent or branch); (3) size of firm; (4) industry (two-digit SIC); (5) site (rural or urban); (6) growth rate, and (7) level of technology. Malizia found that executives from the 39 large establishments placed more emphasis upon land availability/cost, infrastructure availability, livability/education system, and local transportation than did executives from the small establishments (1984:179). For high-technology firms, defined using ten 2-digit SIC codes, the livability/education factor was the most important, followed by local transportation and infrastructure availability. Least important considerations for high-technology firms were land availability/cost, unskilled labor supply, and business taxes/financial considerations (Malizia, 1984:184). However, Malizia's (1984) technology measure suffers from a lack of firm-level information concerning technological sophistication.

Thus, the chief weaknesses of the literature on firm location are fourfold: (1) probability sampling has not been used in selecting firms; samples are usually drawn on a convenience basis; (2) comparisons have not been made by industrial sector; (3) comparisons, to date, have not been made using firm-level measures of technological sophistication; and (4) comparisons omit two basics of organizational form: age and size. If these shortcomings can be remedied, then economic development planners should have a more precise conception of the specific incentives that appeal to different types of firms. Indeed, the absence of a broad-based contingency approach to research on firm location preferences would seem to be a potentially useful explanation of Wolman's (1988) paradox.

Method and Measures

All of this research reported in this chapter draws on data from the Oakland County Business Survey, a five-year longitudinal study of firms in Oakland County, Michigan (Denison and Hart, 1987). The area, known as "Automation Alley," is famous for its high-growth technology corridor interspersed with traditional manufacturing establishments. The sample was selected from the population of all businesses operating from a location in the county as defined by the fourth quarter 1984 ES-202 record of the State of Michigan Employment Security Commissions (MESC). The population included organizations of virtually every type and size, excluding only farms, railroads, and government operations. The use of unemployment insurance records has been shown to be particularly effective as a sampling frame for small and new firms.

The sampling design selected firms with a probability proportional to employment size. This design was used to select a broadly representative sample of 2,248 firms; CEO names and addresses were verified through telephone contact and other sources. Four-digit SIC information from the data-base was used to create two separate strata in the sample: (1) manufacturing and business service firms which were oversampled; and (2) the retail and wholesale sectors, which were undersampled. High-growth firms (based on employment) and corporate headquarters establishments were sampled with certainty to maximize their number.

A questionnaire covering a wide range of issues was mailed to each CEO or firm president (by name) of the 2,248 firms in the sample in June 1986. Following two mail prompts, a second mailing of the questionnaire and extensive follow-up, 665 completed surveys were received for an overall response rate of 30.1 percent. Nonresponse bias was analyzed both with regard to SIC code and employment size. Response rates were quite similar across categories, although larger firms were slightly more likely to respond than smaller firms. And as also might be expected, both the sample and the respondent group were predominantly smaller firms. Forty percent of the respondent firms employed five or fewer employees and 75 percent of the respondent firms employed one hundred or fewer employees.

Dependent variables for this study consisted of a broad range of locational criteria drawn from the literature discussed above. CEOs were asked to rate, on a 1 to 5 scale, the importance of thirty-seven influences on location. The scale measured the degree to which each item was perceived as an incentive or disincentive to locating in Oakland County, with 5 representing a "strong incentive" and 1 a "strong disincentive"; a rating of 3 indicated that the respondent felt that the item was neutral — that it had no real impact on location decision making in the county, as shown in table 12.1. Exploratory factor analysis revealed eight factors, with two additional items retained because of their expected practical and theoretical importance. Indexes were computed by averaging the items that represented each factor. These factors along with their associated items from the instrument mean values and Cronbach alphas are shown in table 12.2.

Using one-way analysis of variance, these ten location factors are examined in relation to four independent variables: (1) age, (2) size, (3) industry sector, and (4) level of technology. Employment size consisted of five levels: (1) 1–5 employees, (2) 6–25 employees, (3) 26–100 employees, (4) 101–500 employees, and (5) >500 employees. Age was bracketed into four categories: (1) 1–5 years, (2) 6–12 years, (3) 13–24 years, and (4) ≥25 years. CEOs were asked to categorize their firms into one of the following six industrial sectors: retail, wholesale, manufacturing, finance and insurance (FIRE), business services, and other services. A total of 516 firms

Table 12.1 Results for Locational Factor Items

How much of an incentive was each of the following factors in your firm or facility's decision to choose your present location or to expand at your present location?

1 Strong Disincentive	2 Moderate Disincentive	3 Neutral	4 Moderate Incentive	5 Strong Incentive

Instrument Item	Mean
b. Proximity to markets/customers	4.3
r. Availability of space and facilities	3.8
aa. Overall quality of the locality	3.8
dd. Proximity to owner's or employees' residences	3.8
cc. Long-term growth potential for the area	3.7
k. Quality of the local environment	3.6
q. Cost of space and facilities	3.6
gg. Quality of roads and highways	3.5
f. Proximity of suppliers/vendors	3.3
ee. Availability of qualified managerial people	3.3
ff. Attitudes of local banking community	3.3
kk. Security	3.3
a. Availability of technical and scientific people	3.2
e. Availability of qualified production workers	3.2
n. Attitude of community toward business	3.2
v. Quality of housing	3.2
m. Proximity to other companies in the same business	3.1
o. Quality of the school system	3.1
t. Availability of educational/training programs	3.1
d. Cultural and entertainment attractions	3.0
i. Access to a university or college	3.0
j. Local zoning and building codes	3.0
s. Quality of health care	3.0
w. Ground transportation system	3.0
y. Convenience to good air transportation	3.0
jj. Availability of funding	3.0
g. Presence of economic development programs	2.9
h. Recreational opportunities	2.9
l. Access to corporate laboratories	2.9
u. Costs of utilities—gas	2.9
x. Costs of utilities—electric	2.9
z. Local wage rates	2.9
c. Local property taxes	2.8
p. Access to government or private laboratories	2.8
bb. Workers' compensation	2.3
hh. Single business tax	2.3
ii. Unemployment compensation	2.2

153

Table 12.2　Location Factor Indexes, with Mean Values, Alphas, and Composite Items

Dimension/ Index	n	Mean	Alpha	Items Included
Sociotechnical infrastructure	544	2.9	0.87	Goverment/private labs; access to university; corporate labs; quality of health care; recreational opportunities; cultural entertainment; economic development programs; availability of managerial people.
Business climate	550	2.9	0.78	Electricity costs; gas costs; availability of funding; wage rates; property taxes.
Overall quality	553	3.7	0.70	Quality of the locality; security; environmental quality; long-term growth potential.
State taxes	550	2.3	0.84	Unemployment compensation; single business tax; workers' compensation.
Commercial space	557	3.5	0.60	Cost of space; availability of space; zoning and building codes.
Housing*	555	3.2	–	Quality of housing.
Transportation	552	3.1	0.61	Convenience to airport; ground transportation; quality of roads and highways.
Input availability	554	3.3	0.65	Proximity to suppliers; availability of scientific and technical people; availability of production workers.
Proximity to markets*	578	4.3	–	Proximity to markets/customers.
Proximity to residence*	561	3.8	–	Proximity to owner's or employees' residences.

Note: An asterisk (*) indicates single item indexes.

responded: 62 in retail, 44 in wholesale, 180 in manufacturing, 60 in finance and insurance, 90 in business services, and 80 in other services.

Two items were used to measure the degree to which firms in the sample were technology-based: (a) the percentage of the annual budget spent on research and development (R&D) and (b) the percentage of employees with scientific and technical training (S&T). The first measure was then split into three categories (no R&D, low R&D, and high R&D) while the second measure was dichotomized (low S&T training or high S&T training), based upon median scores on the two variables. A pattern variable was then created as shown in figure 12.1. Of the firms completing these items, 106 were classified as low tech, 127 were

Figure 12.1: Pattern Variable for Level of Technology

	Low S&T	High S&T
No R&D	Low technology	Medium-low
Low R&D	Medium-low	Medium-high
High R&D	Medium-high	High technology

medium-low tech, 81 were medium-high tech firms and 39 were high-tech firms. Where significant differences occurred among the means, multiple pairwise comparison was employed to test simultaneously for all possible comparisons.

Results

Overall, a handful of items emerged as the major incentives to locating in the county, as depicted in table 12.1. The most important factors appear to be proximity to markets and residences, quality of the local environment, and growth potential for the area. While "quality of life" criteria appear to be very important to all firms locating in this area, several important "least-cost" factors also appear on this list. Proximity to markets/customers and cost of space and facilities are two in particular. Significant, however, is the fact that traditional "smokestack" location criteria, such as utility costs, wage rates, transportation, and taxes, appear to have dropped off the list of primary concerns firms have when it comes to choosing a business location.

Firm Size

As table 12.3 indicates, size has an impact on only three of the ten location factors: (1) Sociotechnical Infrastructure, (2) Proximity to Markets, and (3) Proximity to Residence. Thus, firms of varying size possess approximately the same level of emphasis on seven of the ten location indexes, as presented in Hart, Henderson, and Denison (1989).

Pairwise comparisons heighten differences on the three statistically significant location indexes. Small firms (1–5 employees) and medium-small firms (6–25 employees) place considerably less emphasis on "sociotechnical infrastructure" than do larger firms, suggesting that the area may lack the necessary infrastructure, from their point of view. In contrast, the larger firms (>25 employees) in the sample view sociotechnical infrastructure as a slight incentive. Two groups of firms thus emerge from the analysis of this factor: those with 1–25 employees and those with more than 26 employees.

Table 12.3 Analysis of Variance Results for Ten Location Factors, by Employment Size

Location Factors	Employment Size						
	1-5	6-25	26-100	101-500	>500	N	p
Sociotechnical infrastructure	2.86	2.88	3.02	3.02	3.11	495	.01
Business climate	2.88	2.82	2.87	2.93	3.05	502	.56
Overall quality	3.74	3.66	3.79	3.70	3.73	504	.82
State taxes	2.34	2.30	2.21	2.22	2.47	503	.57
Commercial space	3.50	3.52	3.54	3.55	3.50	508	.98
Housing	3.18	3.14	3.18	3.17	3.45	506	.56
Transportation	3.09	3.04	3.22	3.12	3.10	503	.47
Input availability	3.15	3.25	3.37	3.30	3.30	503	.19
Proximity to markets	4.26	4.21	4.55	4.52	4.35	525	.02
Proximity to residence	4.00	3.72	3.77	3.58	3.65	510	.01

Firms of different sizes also hold distinct views concerning the importance of "proximity to markets" in location decisions. It is least important for small (1–5 employees) and medium-small firms (6–25 employees) and more important for medium-large (26–100 employees) to large firms (101–500 employees). Interestingly, the largest firms (>500 employees) were not statistically different from the very small firms. Medium-sized firms, therefore, appear to be the most concerned about proximity to markets in their location decisions. Differences among firms were also found on the "proximity to residence" factor, with small firms (1–5 employees) indicating proximity to residence as the chief location criteria in firm location. Indeed, small firms are statistically different from all other size groups, including medium-small firms (6–25 employees).

The lack of differences by firm size across the other seven location factors is an important finding in itself: (1) Business Climate, (2) Overall Quality, (3) State Taxes, (4) Commercial Space, (5) Housing, (6) Transportation, and (7) Input Availability all appear to be salient to large and small firms alike.

Firm Age

Even more surprising results (or perhaps nonresults!) were found when firms were defined by age, as shown in table 12.4. Newer firms rank the importance of the various location criteria in much the same order as older firms. For example, new firms consider "proximity to markets" as the primary variable in location decisions, just as old firms do. The only exception to this "no difference" finding is the marginally significant impact of age on "state taxes." These findings are also somewhat difficult to interpret, since they show that "middle aged" firms (6–24 years) see state taxes as the greatest disincentive, while the newest and oldest firms see state taxes as the least disincentive. As Hart, Henderson, and Denison (1989) indicated, these results largely contradict McDermott and Taylor (1976), who found that industrial location preferences varied significantly by firm age. Old firms in McDermott and Taylor's (1976) study exhibited a markedly different set of concerns in their locational preferences. Given probability sampling, results from Michigan's "Automation Alley" do not support the view of age as a good basis for understanding location preferences.

Industrial Sector

Table 12.5 contains the results for the ten location factors across the six industrial sectors. Firms from all industrial sectors appear to value six of the ten location factors equally: (1) Sociotechnical Infrastructure,

Table 12.4 Analysis of Variance Results for Ten Location Factors, by Age

Location Factors	Age Brackets					
	1-5	6-12	13-24	≥25	N	p
Sociotechnical infrastructure	2.94	2.93	2.87	3.00	212	.71
Business climate	2.82	2.84	2.80	2.96	215	.51
Overall quality	3.62	3.60	3.80	3.65	215	.58
State taxes	2.32	2.11	2.00	2.40	214	.07
Commercial space	3.86	3.57	3.47	3.47	216	.59
Housing	3.07	3.29	3.32	3.25	215	.23
Transportation	3.08	3.04	3.02	3.27	214	.22
Input availability	3.24	3.38	3.24	3.33	215	.70
Proximity to markets	4.31	4.26	4.29	4.51	225	.44
Proximity to residence	3.89	4.03	3.81	3.60	217	.11

Table 12.5   Analysis of Variance Results for Ten Location Factors, by Industrial Sector

Location Factors		Industry						
	Retail	Wholesale	Manufacturing	FIRE	Business Services	Other Services	N	p
Sociotechnical infrastructure	2.78	2.82	2.95	2.96	2.94	2.98	531	.24
Business climate	2.80	2.79	2.80	2.90	2.94	2.98	538	.37
Overall quality	3.80	3.74	3.61	4.00	3.71	3.78	540	.03
State taxes	2.29	2.36	2.08	2.62	2.15	2.64	537	.00
Commercial space	3.57	3.52	3.39	3.49	3.58	3.64	544	.27
Housing	2.92	2.95	3.16	3.31	3.27	3.16	542	.02
Transportation	2.94	3.21	3.15	3.17	3.11	3.16	539	.43
Input availability	2.80	3.03	3.52	3.15	3.30	3.13	541	.00
Proximity to markets	4.48	4.38	4.18	4.30	4.33	4.48	565	.23
Proximity to residence	3.59	3.82	3.85	3.78	3.85	3.72	548	.61

(2) Business Climate, (3) Commercial Space, (4) Transportation, (5) Proximity to Markets, and (6) Proximity to Residences. Thus, contrary to what many previous studies suggest, significant differences exist for only four of the ten location factors: (1) Overall Quality, (2) State Taxes, (3) Housing, and (4) Input Availability.

In an effort to pinpoint more directly differences between industry sectors, a set of pairwise comparisons between all sectors were performed for each of the four factors on which significant differences occurred. Detailed statistical results are provided in Hart, Denison, and Henderson (1989). Essentially, the results show that:

- *Retail, Wholesale, and Other Service firms* are most concerned about "proximity to market."
- *Manufacturing firms* value "input availability" more than any other sector. They are also more inclined to see "state taxes" as a disincentive.
- *FIRE firms* are more concerned with "overall quality" of the location and are less concerned with "state taxes" as a disincentive.
- *Business Service firms* place the most emphasis upon "housing" and are also concerned about "input availability."

Level of Technology

Overall, the data indicate that high-technology firms, while similar to other firms in most respects, differ significantly on certain location factors, as shown in table 12.6. Firms of all levels of technology place approximately the same value on eight of the ten location factor indexes: (1) Sociotechnical Infrastructure, (2) Business Climate, (3) Overall Quality, (4) State Taxes, (5) Housing, (6) Transportation, (7) Proximity to Markets, and (8) Proximity to Residence. Significant differences by level of technology are evident for only two of the ten location factors: (1) Commercial Space and (2) Input Availability.

As explained more fully in Hart, Denison, and Henderson (1989), low-technology firms are distinguished by two distinct concerns: they attach greater importance to "commercial space" than other firms, and they place less value than other firms on "input availability." Medium-low- and medium-high-technology firms attach far less importance to commercial space than do low-technology firms, and are higher than low-technology firms in the importance that they attach to input availability. High-technology firms, in particular, emphasize input availability the most while placing the least importance upon commercial space.

Finally, with regard to individual location factor items (see table 12.2), high-technology firms have a distinct preference for areas with access

Table 12.6 Analysis of Variance Results for Ten Location Factors, by Level of Technology

Location Factors	Technology Level				N	p
	Low	Medium Low	Medium High	High		
Sociotechnical infrastructure	2.87	2.95	2.90	3.08	531	.18
Business climate	2.88	2.92	2.81	2.82	538	.65
Overall quality	3.71	3.62	3.58	3.76	540	.51
State taxes	2.19	2.32	2.04	2.34	537	.15
Commercial space	3.69	3.46	3.40	3.26	544	.02
Housing	3.06	3.17	3.19	3.21	542	.51
Transportation	3.08	3.13	3.19	3.08	539	.73
Input availability	3.13	3.45	3.67	3.40	541	.02
Proximity to markets	4.39	4.20	4.38	4.36	565	.46
Proximity to residence	3.82	3.83	3.89	3.95	548	.87

to a university or college, corporate laboratories, and educational programs. Again, given such firms' "knowledge intensity," this result should come as no surprise. What is clear is that the locational preferences for high-technology firms are different in important ways from those of heavy industrial facilities and other organizations putting less emphasis on technological sophistication.

Discussion

The results presented here—a clarification of the differing perceptions and needs regarding location of firms—are important from the perspectives of both theory and practice in economic development. From a theoretical perspective the results suggest that a *contingency theory* of firm location may be necessary to capture the complexity of different types of business organizations. Just as in organization theory, it appears that no single normative theory adequately represents the range of strategies, needs, and values of today's business organizations when it comes to location decisions.

Firms of varying *size,* for example, reveal some important differences with respect to the ten location factors. Results show that in targeting incentives having to do with "sociotechnical infrastructure," a firm having twenty-six employees is statistically indistinguishable from a firm of more than five hundred employees. While very small firms consider sociotechnical infrastructure a disincentive, larger firms view sociotechnical infrastructure more favorably, a situation which probably underscores the traditional bias of development planners toward providing infrastructure incentives predominantly to larger firms. Local economic development planners, recognizing that smaller firms are responsible for most job creation, seem to have not yet resolved smaller firms' needs in regard to sociotechnical infrastructure. Thus, a key distinguishing feature of firms in understanding locational preferences is an employment size of less than twenty-five; beyond this threshold, firms largely consider the same factors in their location preferences.

Important differences also arise across *industry* sector and level of *technology.* In particular, significant differences on the location factors were found with respect to "overall quality," "housing," "state taxes," and "input availability." Understanding these differences and knowing the degree of emphasis placed on each can help economic development planners target more accurately those policies, programs, and incentives that are most likely to be desired by firms from different industrial sectors and with differing levels of technological sophistication. For example, the results reported here indicate that for business service firms, greater emphasis is placed on "housing availability," whereas for manufacturing firms, the most important location criteria relate to "input availability." A single policy toward business attraction and development, particularly if it is oriented primarily toward least-cost factors, would clearly not address the specific interests and needs of these two different types of organizations.

While important contingencies clearly exist, it is also striking how *few* significant differences there are for most locational criteria. Consider the issue of "proximity to markets." Historically, proximity to markets has been suggested as the key location factor for low-technology firms, while high-technology firms presumably value "quality of life" considerations. Firms in this study, however, did not differ significantly on this dimension, whether the population of firms was defined by industrial sector or by level of technology. Similarly, firms from different industrial sectors and levels of technology could not be differentiated on the basis of their orientation toward "proximity to residence," "transportation," "commercial space," "sociotechnical infrastructure," or "business climate."

The results for "state taxes" offer yet another example of the "no difference" finding. Conventional wisdom suggests that smaller, newer firms should view state taxes more as a disincentive in location than would older, larger firms, since, among other things, older firms should be in a stronger position to bear the state tax burden. The results here demonstrate that firms are not significantly different in their view of state taxes whether defined by size or age. In fact, no differences were found on any of the locational criteria for firms on the basis of *age*, and consequently, the hope of targeting incentives based purely on age will probably fall short of the mark.

In all, these results underscore the need to consider simultaneously the private and public incentives that are components of the least-cost and infrastructure views of industrial location. Efforts at new business recruitment and development must be targeted in specific ways, depending on the size, industry, and level of technology of the businesses involved. Local economic development planners need to concentrate, as McDermott and Taylor (1976) pointed out, on providing a wide range of interrelated services, not on public services exclusively, in order to have the greatest impact in industrial decision making. While tax incentives and low-cost schemes were the traditional keys in the game of economic development, the results presented here question the effectiveness of many of these policies and programs (e.g., tax abatements, inexpensive land, and cheap labor). Ultimately, these results should aid in the development of better contingency plans and policies along with more effective incentive schemes for state and local governments.

The results also suggest that there may be regional differences regarding the importance of different location criteria. For example, while "ambiance" was the major location factor for high-technology firms in Orange and San Diego counties in California, a similar set of priorities among high-technology firms in Oakland County, Michigan, (represented by this study) was not observed. Indeed, it may be that there are important cultural and socio-economic differences that dictate an emphasis on one configuration of criteria as opposed to another in different regions. Malecki (1987), Wolman (1988), and Weiss (1988) underscore this point. Further comparative work across nations and regions, especially developed versus developing, is clearly in order since the bulk of research to date has been conducted in the United States, in particular the Silicon Valley and Route 128.

At this point, however, it seems fair to say that the salience of particular location factors varies far more by *geographic region* than it does by type of firm: the preferences of particular types of firms, as shown by this study, are relatively constant. The salience of location factors in different regions, however, seem to vary a great deal, as indicated by the conflicting results from the many studies cited. These differences seem to parallel the underlying strategic intentions of the firms that choose particular locations. The literature on corporate strategy, for example, suggests that there are two differing motives for firms to locate facilities in a particular region (Porter, 1980; Ghoshal, 1987). First, a firm may be seeking to *lower its costs* through economies of scale, factor cost advantages, exchange differentials, or tax policies. This corresponds to the "least-cost" perspective from the economic development literature. Alternatively, a firm may enter a new region to *learn* how to better serve the particular needs of that market. This second motive corresponds closely to the "infrastructure" perspective from the economic development literature, since it implies long-term investment and cultivation of local suppliers and customers. Recognizing these differences and understanding the degree of emphasis placed by firms on each of the location factors can help public managers target more accurately those incentives that best match the real needs of the firms. Indeed, a clearer understanding of firm's strategic intentions may help to clarify Wolman's (1988) paradox: targeting "least-cost" incentives at firms whose strategic intention is to learn how better to respond to regional market needs can only meet with frustration on the part of both parties.

An equally significant issue may be, beyond what firms *prefer* in their location, how firms actually *use* their location. It may be more important for economic development managers to consider the connection that firms establish with the local economy through their networks of input and output linkages. Then, if a categorization of firms in terms of linkage effects were available, development planners could aim for organizational types that were most likely to create regional multiplier effects, or they could seek to develop the necessary infrastructure to encourage particular firms to locate in the area. The connection between how firms use their location (i.e., the network of linkages) and the demand and choice of new industrial locations (i.e., the locational preferences of organizations) can be understood only when the connections between sourcing, job creation, exporting, strategy, growth, and profitability are understood. Future economic development research must focus more directly on these issues.

Notes

1. The Oakland County, Michigan, Department of Economic and Community Development and the School of Business Administration at the University of Michigan provided support for this research.

Contributors

Stephen J. Adams is state economist and director for economic and energy policy with the Maine State Planning Office. He has conducted economic policy research for the state planning office for six years. Prior to working in Maine, Adams was a research analyst with the New York State Senate Research Service in Albany. At the Policy Academy, he served as coach for the Pennsylvania team. He received a Master of Public Administration in Economic Development from Pennsylvania State University.

Stephen Archer is Guy F. Atkinson Professor Finance and Economics at the Atkinson Graduate School of Management, Willamette University. Coauthor of seven texts in the business finance/management area, he also has written numerous articles. He is a former president of the Financial Management Association and prior consultant to states and other local governments on regulatory finance topics.

Barry Bozeman is director of the Technology and Information Policy Program at Syracuse University and professor of public administration. His research is in the areas of science and technology policy and organization theory. Bozeman's most recent book is *Public Management Strategies* (with J. Straussman).

Terry F. Buss is professor and director of the doctoral program in urban studies at the University of Akron. He received his doctoral degree in political science and mathematics from Ohio State University. He has published over one hundred twenty-five articles and ten books on public policy issues. His latest projects involve the study of rural entrepreneurship in the United States and economic development in Hungary.

James C. Clingermayer is an assistant professor in the Department of Political Science at Texas A&M University. His research examines a variety of topics in the fields of urban administration and state regulatory policy. He has published articles in the *Western Political Quarterly, Public Choice,* and *Policy Studies Journal.*

David Coursey is assistant professor in the School of Public Administration and Policy at Florida State University. His research interests include political economy, research and development policy, and management information systems. He received his doctorate from the Maxwell School at Syracuse University.

Daniel R. Denison is assistant professor of organizational behavior at the University of Michigan's Graduate School of Business. His primary research interest is organizational culture and effectiveness and the impact that human resources management has on productivity and performance.

Rodney A. Erickson is professor of business administration and geography at The Pennsylvania State University, where he has been a member of the faculty since 1977. He serves as director of the Center for Regional Business Analysis in the Smeal College of Business Administration and head of the Department of Geography in the College of Earth and Mineral Sciences. Erickson earned his Ph.D. at the University of Washington in 1973 and was previously on the faculty at the University of Wisconsin–Madison. He is the author of more than one hundred articles, book chapters, monographs, and professional papers dealing with regional economic growth theory and models, economic development policies, and the geography of international business.

Richard C. Feiock is an associate professor in the School of Public Administration at Florida State University. His research interests include local economic development policy, municipal service distribution, and state environmental regulation. His articles have appeared in the *American Journal of Political Science, Western Political Quarterly, Public Administration Quarterly, Review of Public Personnel Administration,* and other scholarly journals.

Richard L. Gardner has served as a policy economist in the Idaho Division of Financial Management in the executive office of the governor for the past eight years. His work currently focuses on rural development. He was a member of the governor's Rural Policy Working Group and currently co-chairs the interagency Idaho Rural Development Council. In the Rural Policy Academy, he served as coach for the North Dakota team. Gardner has published extensively on a broad range of policy topics and writes a monthly newsletter on the Idaho economy called the *Idaho Outlook.* He received an M.S. in Resource Economics from the University of Minnesota and a Ph.D. in Agricultural and Resource Economics from Colorado State University.

Ruth M. Grubel is an associate professor of political science at the University of Wisconsin–Whitewater. She has received several grants to research intergovernmental relations in trade policy and is now investigating sources of information and assistance for businesses exporting to Japan. In addition to courses in Public Administration, she teaches a class on U.S.–Japan relations. She was awarded a Fulbright lecturing grant at Hiroshima University, Japan, for 1991-92.

Stuart L. Hart is assistant professor of corporate strategy and organizational behavior at the University of Michigan Graduate School of Business Administration. His interests center on the strategy making and management processes of technology-based organizations.

Douglas A. Henderson earned a Ph.D. from the University of Michigan and is currently a law clerk with Reeves & Graddy in Lexington and Versailles, Kentucky. His interests include natural resources law, environmental science, and economic development.

Craig R. Humphrey is associate professor of sociology at The Pennsylvania State University (University Park). Mr. Humphrey's scholarly interests include the organizational responses of cities and towns in the northeastern United States to deindustrialization and economic restructuring and the sociology of natural resources. In an effort to combine these interests, he currently is engaged in research on local economic development efforts and their consequences for communities in a forested region of the Northeast. He is also the chairperson of the Subcommittee on Natural Resources and Poverty, Rural Sociological Society Task Force on the Persistence of Poverty in America. He earned his Ph.D. from Brown University.

Steven Maser is professor of public management and public policy at the Atkinson Graduate School of Management, Willamette University. His published research includes studies of municipal zoning, urban government, and transaction cost analyses of constitutions and public policies. With Stephen Archer, he designed and executed an International Trade Institute for state government officials in the Northwest.

Robert P. McGowan is associate professor of management in the College of Business, University of Denver, where he specializes in public policy and business and corporate strategy. He has published articles in such journals as *Policy Studies Journal*, *Policy Studies Review*, and *Public Administration Review* and is currently researching in the area of international strategic alliances.

Edward J. Ottensmeyer holds M.B.A. and Ph.D. degrees from Indiana University and is an assistant professor in the Graduate School of Management at Clark University. Prior to joining the Clark faculty in 1986, he served on the business school faculties of The Pennsylvania State University and the University of Denver. His additional work experience includes six years of planning and policy analysis in the public sector. His research on managing strategic issues has appeared in the *Academy of Management Review*, *Business Horizons*, and the *Journal of Business Ethics*. His work on economic development strategy has been published in *Policy Studies Review*, *Policy Studies Journal*, *Growth and Change*, and *Economic Development Commentary*.

John M. Redman is senior economist with the Government and Development Policy Section of the Economic Research Service. His research focuses on issues related to state and federal economic development policy. Previously, Redman worked for a number of private research and consulting firms specializing in federal policy and regulatory analysis. He also served on the staff of a U.S. Senate committee, where he worked on economic development policy issues. He has a B.S. in International Affairs from the School of Foreign Service, Georgetown University, and an M.S. in Agricultural Economics from the University of Wisconsin–Madison.

David W. Sears is head of the Government and Development Policy (GDP) Section in the Economic Research Service. The GDP Section conducts a wide variety of policy-relevant research projects aimed at examining approaches that might stimulate rural development or overcome barriers to rural development. He joined ERS in 1988 after many years in a variety of federal government research and evaluation offices, including those examining the UDAG and CDBG programs. Sears earned his M.P.A. (public administration) and Ph.D. (city and regional planning) from Cornell, and taught for several years in the Regional Planning program at the University of Massachusetts at Amherst.

Roger J. Vaughan is president of Roger Vaughan Associates, an economic development consulting firm, and visiting professor of economics at the University of Akron. He received his doctoral degree in economics from the University of Chicago. He has made major contributions to the field of economic development and is best known for his book *The Wealth of States* (1984). He is currently working in five states on education reform.

William L. Waugh, Jr., is an associate professor of public administration, political science, and urban studies at Georgia State University. He is the author of *Terrorism and Emergency Management* (1990) and *International Terrorism* (1982) and coeditor of *Cities and Disaster: North American Studies in Emergency Management* (1990), the *Handbook of Emergency Management* (1990), and *Anti-Terrorism Policies: An International Comparison* (1991). He has also written numerous articles and chapters on economic development, emergency management, decision making, and local government published in the United States, Canada, and Western Europe. He is chair-elect of the American Society for Public Administration's Section on Emergency Management and serves on the executive board of the American Political Science Association's Section on Public Administration.

Scott A. Woodard is an independent consultant in Denver, Colorado, specializing in strategic management and organization development for an array of public sector and not-for-profit organizations. He has worked with Colorado's community colleges to define their roles in the state's economic development and workforce initiatives. Earlier, he developed strategies for economic development and education and training for the Governor's Office of Planning and Budgeting. Woodard is a doctoral student in the Graduate School of Public Affairs at the University of Colorado, Denver. His major area of interest is the application of strategic planning to public management.

References

Chapter 1: Emerging Issues in Economic Development

Beaumont, E.F., and H.A. Hovey. 1985. "State, Local and Federal Economic Development Policies: New Federal Patterns, Chaos, or What?" *Public Administration Review* 45 (2):327–340.

Corporation for Enterprise Development. 1988. *Report Card on the States.* Washington, D.C.: Corporation for Enterprise Development.

Grady, Dennis O. 1987. "State Economic Development: Why Do States Compete?" *State and Local Government Review* 19:86–94.

Morrison, Catherine, E. Patrick McQuire, and M.A. Clark. 1988. *Keys to U.S. Competitiveness.* New York: Conference Board.

National Alliance of Business. 1987. *Employing Human Capital: To Achieve Priority Economic Development Objectives.* Washington, D.C.: National Alliance of Business.

Steinnes, Donald N. 1984. "Business Climate, Tax Incentives, and Regional Economic Development." *Growth and Change* 15:38–47.

U.S. Office of Technology Assessment. 1984. *Technology, Innovation and Regional Economic Development.* Background Paper no. 2. Washington, D.C.: U.S. Congress.

Chapter 2: University-Industry Cooperative R&D

Abelson, P. 1988. "Academic-Industrial Interactions." *Science,* 240:265.

Anthes, G. 1991. "U.S. Budget Shines on High-Tech." *Computerworld* 25(6):90.

Biddle, W. 1987. "Corporations on Campus." *Science* 237:353–355.

Bozeman, B., and M. Crow. In press. "Pork Barrel, Peer Review and Congressional Science Policy." *Forum* 6.

———. 1990. "The Environments of U.S. R&D Laboratories: Political and Market Influences." *Policy Sciences* 23:25–56.

Bozeman, B., and A. Link. 1984. Tax Incentives for R&D: A Critical Evaluation. *Research Policy* 13:21–31.

Culliton, B. 1990. "Stanford Psychiatry Deal Falls Through." *Science* 247:1404.

Fowler, D. 1984. "University-Industry Research Relationships." *Research Management* 27(1):35–41.

Gander, J. 1986. "The Economics of University-Industry Research Linkages." *Technological Forecasting and Social Change* 29:33–49.

Gray, P. 1990. "Advantageous Liaisons." *Issues in Science and Technology* 6(3):40–46.

Hamilton, D. 1990. "Magnet Lab: Science to the Highest Bidder?" *Science* 249:851.

Jones, M. 1989. "Helping States Help Themselves." *Issues in Science and Technology* 6(1):56–60.

Lambright, H., and A. Teich. 1989. "Science, Technology, and State Economic Development." *Policy Studies Journal* 18:135–147.

Lambright, H., and D. Rahm. 1990. *Science, Technology, and the American States.* Paper presented at the meeting of the Southeastern Conference of Public Administration, Clearwater Beach, Fla.

Link, A., and L. Bauer. 1989. *Cooperative Research in U.S. Manufacturing: Assessing Policy Initiatives and Corporate Strategies.* Lexington, Mass: Lexington Books.

McHenry, K. 1990. "Five Myths of Industry/University Cooperative Research—and the Realities." *Research Technology Management* 33(3):40–42.

Minnesota Department of Trade and Economic Development. 1988. *State Technology Programs in the United States.* St. Paul: Minnesota Office of Science and Technology.

Norman, C. 1990. "MIT Tenure Case Heads to Trial." *Science* 247:1536.

Osborne, D. 1988. *Laboratories of Democracy.* Boston: Harvard Business School Press.

Rahm, D. 1989. "Federal Efforts to Enhance U.S. International Competitiveness: The Encouragement of Domestic Cooperation." *Policy Studies Journal* 18:89–97.

"The Research and Expenditure Tax Credit." 1990. *Research Technology Management* 33(1):5.

Rousch, W. 1990. "Science and Technology in the 101st Congress." *Technology Review* 93(8):59–69.

Smilor, R., and D. Gibson. 1991. Accelerating Technology Transfer in R&D Consortia. *Research Technology Management* 34(1):44–49.

Wolff, M. 1989. "California Spends Most on Industrial R&D." *Research Technology Management* 32(2):3–5.

Chapter 3: Trade, Economic Growth, and State Export Promotion Programs

Archer, Stephen H., and Steven M. Maser. 1989. "State Export Promotion for Economic Development." *Economic Development Quarterly* 3:235–242.

Armington, Paul. 1969. "A Theory of Demand for Products Distinguished by Place of Production." *International Monetary Fund Staff Papers* 16:159–178.

Berry, Willard M., and William A. Mussen. 1980. Part I. In *Export Development and Foreign Investment: The Role of the States and Its Linkage to Federal Action.* Committee on International Trade and Foreign Relations. Washington, D.C.: National Governors' Association.

Coughlin, Cletis C., and Phillip A. Cartwright. 1987a. "An Examination of State Foreign Export Promotion and Manufacturing Exports." *Journal of Regional Science* 27:439–449.

———. 1987b. "An Examination of State Foreign Exports and Manufacturing Employment." *Economic Development Quarterly* 1:257–267.

Erickson, Rodney A. 1989. "Export Performance and State Industrial Growth." *Economic Geography* 65:280–292.

———, and David J. Hayward. 1991a. "The International Flows of Industrial Exports from U.S. Regions." *Annals of the Association of American Geographers* 81, forthcoming.

———. 1991b. "Interstate Differences in Relative Export Performance: A Test of Factor Endowments Theory." Paper presented at the Annual Meeting of the Association of American Geographers, Miami, Fla.

Farrell, Michael G., and Anthony Radspieler. 1989. "Census Bureau State-by-State Foreign Trade Data: Historical Perspective; Current Situation; Future Outlook." Paper presented to the National Governors' Association, Committee on International Trade and Foreign Relations, Washington, D.C.

Fieleke, Norman S. 1986. "New England Manufacturing and International Trade." *New England Economic Review* (Sept./Oct.):22–28.

Florida Department of Commerce. 1989. *The Impact of Foreign Trade on Florida's Economy.* Tallahassee, Fla: Florida Department of Commerce.

Gillespie, Robert W. 1982. "The Midwest Region and the International Economy." In *The Midwest Economy: Issues and Policy,* edited by R. W. Resek and R. F. Kosobud. Urbana: University of Illinois, pp. 185–211.

Griffin, Adrian H. 1989. *California Exports: Their Contribution to the Economy.* Sacramento: California Department of Commerce.

Hanink, Dean M. 1987. "A Comparative Analysis of the Competitive Geographical Trade Performances of the USA, FRG, and Japan: The Markets and Marketers Hypothesis." *Economic Geography* 63:293–305.

———. 1988. "An Extended Linder Model of International Trade." *Economic Geography* 64:322–334.

Hayter, Roger M. 1986. "Export Performance and Export Potentials: Western Canadian Exports of Manufactured End Products." *Canadian Geographer* 30:26–39.

Hirsch, Seev. 1971. *The Export Performance of Six Manufacturing Industries.* New York: Praeger.

Krugman, Paul. 1980. "Scale Economies, Product Differentiation, and the Pattern of Trade." *American Economic Review* 70:950–959.

Kudrle, Robert T., and Cynthia M. Kite. 1989. "The Evaluation of State Programs for International Business Development." *Economic Development Quarterly* 3:288–300.

LeHeron, Richard L. 1980. "Exports and Linkage Development in Manufacturing Firms: The Example of Export Promotion in New Zealand." *Economic Geography* 56:281–299.

Markusen, Ann R., Helzi Noponen, and Karl Driessen. 1991. "International Trade, Productivity and Regional Job Growth: A Shift-Share Interpretation." *International Regional Science Review* 14, forthcoming.

McConnell, James E. 1979. "The Export Decision: An Empirical Study of Firm Behavior." *Economic Geography* 55:171–183.

McConnell, James E. 1982. "The Internationalization Process and Spatial Form." *Environment and Planning A* 14:1633–1644.

Namiki, Nobuaki. 1988. "Export Strategy for Small Business." *Journal of Small Business Management* 26:32–37.

National Association of State Development Agencies. 1984. *State Export Promotion Database.* Washington, D.C.: National Association of State Development Agencies.

———. 1986. *State Export Promotion Database.* Washington, D.C.: National Association of State Development Agencies.

———. 1988. *State Export Promotion Database.* Washington, D.C.: National Association of State Development Agencies.

———. 1991. *1990 State Export Promotion Database.* Washington, D.C.: National Association of State Development Agencies.

Norman, George. 1986. "Market Strategy with Variable Entry Threats." In *Spatial Pricing and Differentiated Markets,* edited by G. Norman. London: Pion.

Posner, Alan R. 1984. *State Government Export Promotion.* Westport, Conn.: Quorum Books.

Simpson, C. L., and D. Kujawa. 1974. "The Export Decision Process: An Empirical Inquiry." *Journal of International Business Studies* 5:107–117.

Smith, Tim R. 1989. "Regional Exports of Manufactured Products." *Economic Review* (Federal Reserve Bank of Kansas City) 74(1):21–28.

Suzman, Cedric L., and Lawrence H. Wortzel. 1984. "Technology Profiles and Export Marketing Strategies." *Journal of Business Research* 12:183–194.

U.S. Bureau of Economic Analysis. 1991. "National Income and Product Accounts." *Survey of Current Business* 71 (April):8–23.

U.S. Bureau of the Census. 1990. *Statistical Abstract of the United States: 1990.* Washington, D.C.: U.S. Government Printing Office.

Webster, Elaine, Edward J. Mathis, and Charles E. Zech. 1990. "The Case for State-Level Export Promotion Assistance: A Comparison of Foreign and Domestic Export Employment Multipliers. *Economic Development Quarterly* 4:203–210.

Chapter 4: Government Efforts to Promote International Trade

Anton, T. 1987. "Economic Development, Employment and Training Policy and Federalism." *Policy Studies Review* 6:728–732.

Archer, S., and S. Maser. 1989. "State Export Promotion for Economic Development." *Economic Development Quarterly* 3:235–242.

Bauer, R., I. Pool, and L. Dexter. 1972. *American Business & Public Policy: The Politics of Foreign Trade,* 2d ed. Chicago: Aldine-Atherton.

Bergsten, C. F., and W. Cline. 1987. *The United States-Japan Economic Problem.* Washington, D.C.: Institute for International Economics.

Brauchli, M. W. 1991 (Jan. 24). "Japan's Economic Boom May Be Ending." *Wall Street Journal*, p. A6.

Burgess, J. 1988 (March 7-13). "America on the Block." *Washington Post National Weekly Edition*, pp. 6, 7.

Clayton, M. 1988 (June 30). "Trade Deficit Starts on Factory Floor." *Christian Science Monitor*, p. 16.

Destler, I. M. 1986. *American Trade Politics: System Under Stress*. Washington, D.C.: Institute for International Economics.

———. 1980. *Making Foreign Economic Policy*. Washington, D.C.: Brookings Institution.

———, and J. Odell. 1987. *Anti-Protection: Changing Forces in United States Trade Politics*. Washington, D.C.: Institute for International Economics.

———, and H. Sato. 1982. *Coping with U.S.-Japanese Economic Conflicts*. Lexington, Mass.: Lexington Books.

———, H. Sato, P. Clapp, and H. Fukui. 1976. *Managing an Alliance: The Politics of U.S.-Japanese Relations*. Washington, D.C.: Brookings Institution.

"Foreign Control of Assets in U.S. Rising, Study Says. 1988. (July 28). *Wall Street Journal*, p. 6.

Franck, T., and E. Weisband. 1979. *Foreign Policy by Congress*. New York: Oxford University Press.

Fried, E., P. Trezise, and S. Yoshida. 1983. *The Future Course of U.S.-Japan Economic Relations*. Washington, D.C.: Brookings Institution.

Grady, D. 1987. "State Economic Development Incentives: Why Do States Compete? *State and Local Government Review* 19:86-94.

"Japan's Clout in the U.S." 1988 (July 11). *Business Week*, pp. 64-75.

Kincaid, J. 1984. "The American Governors in International Affairs." *Publius: The Journal of Federalism* 14:95-114.

Kline, J. 1984. "The Expanding International Agenda for State Governments." *State Government* 57:2-6.

———. 1983. *State Government Influence in U.S. International Economic Policy*. Lexington, Mass.: Lexington Books.

Lincoln, E. 1988. *Japan: Facing Economic Maturity*. Washington, D.C.: Brookings Institution.

Morin, R. 1988 (May 16-22). "Maybe We're Chasing After the Wrong 'Evil Empire.' " *Washington Post National Weekly Edition*, p. 34.

National Association of State Development Agencies. 1991, 1986, 1984. *NASDA State Export Program Database*. Washington, D.C.: NASDA.

Neuse, S. 1982. "State Activities in International Trade." *State Government* 55:57-64.

Norman, J. 1991 (March 7). "Weak Dollar to Force Cuts at Trade Offices." *Milwaukee Journal*, p. C8.

Pastor, R. 1980. *Congress and the Politics of U.S. Foreign Economic Policy, 1929-1976*. Berkeley: University of California Press.

Pilcher, D. 1985 (April). "State Roles in Foreign Trade." *State Legislatures*, pp. 18-23.

Prestowitz, C.V., Jr. 1988. *Trading Places: How We Allowed Japan to Take the Lead*. New York: Basic Books.

Ripley, R., and G. Franklin. 1976. *Congress, the Bureaucracy, and Public Policy*. Homewood, Ill.: Dorsey Press.

Saikowski, C. 1988 (July 27). "Voters' Evolving Security Views." *Christian Science Monitor*, pp. 3, 4.

Scherer, R. 1988 (March 21). "Cheap Dollars Come Home." *Christian Science Monitor*, p. 1.

"Senate Sends the Massive Trade Measure to Reagan after Approving Bill by Resounding Vote of 85-11." 1988 (Aug. 4). *Wall Street Journal*, p. 3.

Tsurumi, Y. 1987. "The U.S. Trade Deficit with Japan." *World Policy Journal* 4:207–230.

U.S. House of Representatives. 1984. *United States-Japan Relations:* Hearings before the Subcommittees on Asian and Pacific Affairs and on International Economic Policy and Trade of the Committee on Foreign Affairs, May 2, 3, 23; June 12.

Chapter 5: Promoting Exports for State Economic Development

Archer, Stephen and Steven Maser. 1989. "State Export Promotion for Economic Development." *Economic Development Quarterly* 3(3).

Council of State Governments. 1983. *State Elective Officials and Legislatures, 1983–84.* Lexington, Ky.: Council of State Governments.

Czinkota, Michael R. 1982. *Export Development Strategies: U.S. Promotion Policies.* New York: Praeger.

Egan, Mary L., and Marc Bendick, Jr. 1985. *The Role of Publicly-Based Export Trading Companies in Reducing Unemployment and Economic Distress.* Washington, D.C.: Department of Commerce, Economic Development Administration.

Guisinger, Stephen E., and Associates. 1985. *Investment Incentives and Performance Requirements.* New York: Praeger.

Kline, John M. 1982. *State Government Influence in U.S. International Economic Policy.* Lexington, Mass.: Lexington Books.

National Governors' Association. 1985. *States in the International Economy.* Washington, D.C.: National Governors' Association.

National League of Cities. 1984. *International Trade: A New City Economic Development Strategy.* Washington, D.C.: National League of Cities.

Neuse, Steven M. 1982. "State Activities in International Trade." *State Government* 55(2).

O'Grady, Dennis O. 1987. "State Economic Development Incentives: Why Do States Compete?" *State and Local Government Review* 19(3).

Peretz, Paul. 1985. "The Market for Industry: Where Angels Fear to Tread." *Policy Studies Review* 5(3).

Pilcher, Daniel E., and Lanny Proffer. 1985. *The States and International Trade: New Roles in Export Development: A Legislator's Guide.* Washington, D.C.: National Conference of State Legislatures.

Price Waterhouse. 1986. *Strategies for Developing Effective State International Business Development Programs.* Washington, D.C.: Department of Commerce, Economic Development Administration.

U.S. Small Business Administration. 1983. *The State of Small Business: A Report of the President.* Washington, D.C.: Small Business Administration.

U.S. Bureau of Census. 1984a. *1984 Annual Survey of Manufacturers.* Washington, D.C.: Bureau of Census.

_____. 1984b. *United States Foreign Trade: U.S. Waterborne Exports and General Imports, 1983.* Washington, D.C: Bureau of Census.

_____. 1986. *State and Metropolitan Area Data Book, 1986.* Washington, D.C.: Bureau of Census.

_____. 1987. *Statistical Abstract of the United States, 1987,* Washington, D.C.: Bureau of Census.

Chapter 7: Designing Successful State Rural Development Strategies

Bartik, Timothy. 1990 (Nov.). "The Market Failure Approach to Regional Economic Development Policy." *Economic Development Quarterly* 4(4).

Clarke, Marianne. 1986. *Revitalizing State Economies.* Washington, D.C.: National Governors' Association.

Corporation for Enterprise Development. N.d. *The Entrepreneurial Economy Review,* 9(1).

Eisner, Robert. 1991. "Our Real Deficits." *American Planning Association Journal* (Spring).

John, Dewitt, Sandra Batie, and Kim Norris. 1988. *A Brighter Future for Rural America: Strategies for Communities and State.* Washington, D.C.: National Governors' Association.

National Governors' Association. 1991. *Excellence at Work: A State Action Agenda.* Washington, D.C.: National Governors' Association.

National Governors' Association. 1988. *New Alliances for Rural America: Report of the Task Force on Rural Development.* Washington, D.C.: National Governors' Association.

Osborne, David. 1988. *Laboratories of Democracy.* Boston: Harvard Business School Press.

Shaffer, Ron. 1990. "Building Economically Viable Communities: A Role for Community Developers." *Journal of the Community Development Society* 21(2).

Vaughan, Roger J., Robert Pollard, and Barbara Dyer. 1984. *The Wealth of States: Policies for a Dynamic Economy.* Washington, D.C.: The Council of State Policy and Planning Agencies.

Chapter 8: Institutional Power and the Art of the Deal

Cassel, Carol. 1986. "The Nonpartisan Ballot in the United States." In *Electoral Laws and Their Political Consequences,* edited by B. Grofman and A. Lijphart. New York: Agathon Press.

Danielson, Michael N., and Jameson W. Doig. 1982. *New York: The Politics of Urban and Regional Development.* Berkeley: University of California Press.

Engstrom, Richard L., and Michael D. McDonald. 1986. "The Effect of At-Large Versus District Elections on Racial Representation in U.S. Municipalities." In *Electoral Laws and their Political Consequences,* edited by B. Grofman and A. Lijphart. New York: Agathon Press.

Fainstein, Susan, and Norman Fainstein, eds. 1986. *Restructuring the City.* New York: Longman.

Feiock, Richard C. 1985. "Local Government Policy and Urban Economic Development." Unpublished doctoral dissertation. Department of Political Science, University of Kansas, Lawrence.

———, and James C. Clingermayer. 1986. "Municipal Representation, Executive Power and Economic Development Policy Adoption." *Policy Studies Journal* 15:211–230.

———. 1988. "Local Government Adoption of Four Economic Development Policy Instruments." Paper presented at the annual meeting of the Southern Political Science Assn.

Ferman, Barbara. 1985. *Governing the Ungovernable City: Political Skill, Leadership, and the Modern Mayor.* Philadelphia, Penn.: Temple University Press.

Fisher, Peter. 1985. "Corporate Tax Incentives: The American Version of Industrial Policy." *Journal of Economic Issues* 19 (March):1–19.

Fosler, R. Scott, and Renee A. Berger. 1982. *Public-Private Partnerships in American Cities: Seven Case Studies.* Lexington, Mass.: Lexington Books.

Frieden, Bernard, and Lynne Sagalyn. 1989. *Downtown, Inc.* Cambridge, Mass.: MIT Press.

Friedland, Roger. 1983. *Power and Crises in the City: Corporations, Unions, and Urban Policy.* New York: Schoken Books.

Hienstand, Dale L. 1979. "Strategic Issues in Local Economic Development." In *Central City Economic Development,* edited by Benjamin Chinitz. Boston, Mass.: Abt Books.

Lineberry, Robert L., and Edmund Fowler. 1967. "Reformism and Public Policies in American Cities." *American Political Science Review* 61:701–716.

Mollenkopf, John. 1983. *The Contested City.* Princeton, N.J.: Princeton University Press.

Molotch, Harvey. 1976. "The City as a Growth Machine." *American Journal of Sociology* 75:309–330.

Premus, Robert. 1984. "Urban Growth and Technological Innovation." In *Urban Economic Development Policy,* edited by Richard Bingham and John Blair. Beverly Hills, Calif.: Sage.

Pressman, Jeffrey L. 1972. "Preconditions of Mayoral Leadership." *American Political Science Review* 66(2) (June):511–524.

Protasel, Greg J. 1988. "Abandonments of the Council-Manager Plan: A New Institutionalist Perspective." *Public Administration Review* 48 (July/Aug.):807–812.

Rubin, Herbert, and Irene Rubin. 1987. "Economic Development Incentives: the Poor (Cities) Pay More." *Urban Affairs Quarterly* 23 (Sept.):37–62.

Schumaker, Paul D., John M. Bolland, and Richard C. Feiock. 1986. "Urban Economic Development and Community Conflict: A Cross-Issue Analysis." In *Research in Urban Policy,* vol. 2, edited by T. Clark. Greenwich, Conn.: JAI Press.

Sharp, Elaine B. 1991. "Institutional Manifestations of Accessibility and Urban Economic Development Policy." *Western Political Quarterly* 44(1) (March):129–147.

Sofen, Edward. 1966. "Quest for Leadership: Strengthening the Mayor's Hands." *National Civic Review* 57:346–351.

Spindler, Charles J., and John P. Forrester. 1991. "Modeling Economic Development Policy: Toward a Political Economy Perspective." Paper presented at the annual meeting of the Urban Affairs Assn., Vancouver, Canada.

Stone, Clarence, and Heywood Sanders. 1987. "Reexamining a Classic Case of Development Politics: New Haven, Connecticut." In *The Politics of Urban Development*, edited by Stone and Sanders. Lawrence: University Press of Kansas.

Swanstrom, Todd. 1985. *The Crises of Growth Politics: Cleveland, Kucinich, and the Challenge of Urban Populism*. Philadelphia, Penn.: Temple University Press.

United States, Department of Housing and Urban Development. 1979. *Economic Guidebook for Local Government*. Washington, D.C.: U.S. Government Printing Office.

Wasylenko, Michael. 1981. "The Location of Firms: The Role of Taxes and Fiscal Incentives." In *Urban Government Finance*, edited by Roy Bahl. Beverly Hills, Calif.: Sage.

Young, Almah. 1984. "Urban Development Action Grants: The New Orleans Experience." *Public Administration Quarterly* 8(1) (Spring):112–119.

Chapter 9: Industrial Development Groups, Local Dependence, and the Community Growth Machine

Alberts, R. C. 1981. *The Shaping of the Point: Pittsburgh's Renaissance Park*. Pittsburgh, Penn.: University of Pittsburgh Press.

Bluestone, Barry, and Bennett Harrison. 1982. *The Deindustrialization of America: Plant Closings, Community Abandonment, and the Dismantling of Basic Industry*. New York: Basic Books.

Castells, Manuel. 1989. *The Informational City: Information Technology, Restructuring, and the Urban-Regional Process*. Oxford, UK: Basil Blackwell.

Cobb, James C. 1982. *The Selling of the South: The Southern Crusade for Industrial Development 1936–1980*. Baton Rouge: Louisiana State University Press.

Cox, Kevin R., and Andrew Mair. 1988. "Locality and Community in the Politics of Local Economic Development." *Annals of the Association of American Geographers* 78:307–325.

_____. 1989. "Review of *Urban Fortunes: the Political Economy of Place* by John Logan and Harvey Molotch." *International Journal of Urban and Regional Research* 13:137–146.

_____. 1991. "From Localised Social Structures to Localities as Agents." *Environment and Planning A* 23:197–213.

Duncan, S., and M. Savage. 1989. "Space, Scale, and Locality." *Antipode* 21:179–206.

Edelstein, Michael R. 1988. *Contaminated Communities: The Social and Psychological Impacts of Residential Toxic Exposure*. Boulder, Colo.: Westview Press.

Erickson, Rodney A., Craig R. Humphrey, and Edward J. Ottensmeyer. 1987. *Not-For-Profit Local Industrial Development Groups: Their Organization, Strategic Activities, and Effectiveness*. Final Report to the Economic Development Administration, U.S. Department of Commerce. Washington, D.C.

Erickson, Rodney A., and David R. Wollover. 1987. "Local Tax Burdens and the Supply of Business Sites in Suburban Municipalities." *Journal of Regional Science* 27:25–37.

Fainstein, Susan S., and Norman Fainstein. 1989. "Economic Development Policy in the U.S. Federal System under the Reagan Administration." *Urban Affairs Quarterly* 25:41–62.

Feagin, Joe R. 1985. "The Global Context of Metropolitan Growth: Houston and the Oil Industry." *American Journal of Sociology* 90:1204–1230.

_____. 1988. *Free Enterprise City.* New Brunswick, N.J.: Rutgers University Press.

Fitzgerald, J. 1991. "Class as Community: The New Dynamics of Social Change." *Environment and Planning D: Society and Space* 9:117–128.

Fleischmann, Arnold, and Joe R. Feagin. 1988. "The Politics of Growth-Oriented Urban Alliances: Comparing Old Industrial and New Sunbelt Cities." *Urban Affairs Quarterly* 23:207–232.

Fosler, R. Scott, and Renee A. Berger, eds. 1982. *Public-Private Partnerships in American Cities.* Lexington, Mass.: D.C. Heath.

Friedland, Roger. 1983. *Power and Crisis in the City.* New York: Macmillan.

Galaskiewicz, Joseph. 1985. *Social Organization of an Urban Grants Economy.* New York: Academic Press.

Goodman, Robert. 1979. *The Last Entrepreneurs: America's Regional Wars for Jobs and Dollars.* New York: Simon and Schuster.

Gottdiener, Mark. 1977. *Planned Sprawl: Private and Public Interests in Suburbia.* Beverly Hills, Calif.: Sage.

_____. 1985. *The Social Production of Urban Space.* Austin: University of Texas Press.

Green, Gary P., and Arnold Fleischmann. 1979. "Analyzing Local Strategies for Promoting Economic Development." *Policy Studies Journal* 17:557–573.

Gregson, N. 1987. "The CURS Initiative: Some Further Comments." *Antipode* 19:364–370.

Hall, Peter. 1987. "Regions in the Transition to the Information Economy." Unpublished paper presented at Rutgers University Conference on America's New Economic Geography. Washington, D.C., April.

Harrison, Bennett. 1984. "Regional Restructuring and Good Business Climates: The Economic Transformation of New England since World War II." In *Sunbelt/Snowbelt: Urban Development and Regional Restructuring,* edited by Larry Sawers and William K. Tabb, New York: Oxford University Press.

_____, and Barry Bluestone. 1988. *The Great U-Turn. Corporate Restructuring and the Polarizing of America.* New York: Basic Books.

Hartman, Chester. 1984. *The Transformation of San Francisco.* Totowa, N.J.: Rowman & Allanheld.

Humphrey, Craig R., Rodney A. Erickson, and Edward J. Ottensmeyer. 1988. "Industrial Development Groups, Organizational Resources, and the Prospects for Effecting Growth in Local Economies." *Growth and Change* 19:1–21.

_____. 1989. "Industrial Development Organizations and the Local Dependence Hypothesis." *Policy Studies Journal* 17:624–642.

_____, Rodney A. Erickson, and Richard E. McCluskey. 1989. "Industrial Development Groups, External Connections, and Job Generation in Local Communities." *Economic Development Quarterly* 3:32–45.

Levine, Adeline G. 1982. *Love Canal: Science, Politics, and People.* Boston, Mass.: Lexington Books.

Logan, John. 1976a. "Industrialization and the Stratification of Cities in Suburban Regions." *American Journal of Sociology* 82:333–348.

———. 1976b. "Notes on the Growth Machine—Toward a Comparative Political Economy of Place." *American Journal of Sociology* 82:349–352.

———, and Reid M. Golden. 1986. "Suburbs and Satellites: Two Decades of Change." *American Sociological Review* 51:430–437.

———, and Harvey Molotch. 1987. *Urban Fortunes: The Political Economy of Place.* Berkeley: University of California Press.

Lubove, Roy. 1969. *Twentieth Century Pittsburgh: Government, Business, and Environmental Change.* New York: Wiley.

Malmberg, Bo. 1990. *The Effects of External Ownership. A Study of Linkages and Branch Plant Location.* Geografisa Regionstudier Nr. 24. Uppsala, Sweden: University of Uppsala Institute of Cultural Geography.

Markusen, Ann R. 1987. *Regions: The Economics and Politics of Territory.* Totowa, N.J.: Rowman and Littlefield.

Molotch, Harvey. 1970. "Oil in Santa Barbara and Power in America." *Sociological Inquiry* 40:131–144.

———. 1976a. "The City as a Growth Machine: Toward a Political Economy of Place." *American Journal of Sociology* 82:309–332.

———. 1976b. "Varieties of Growth Strategy: Some Comments on Logan." *American Journal of Sociology* 82:352–355.

———, and John Logan. 1984. "Tensions in the Growth Machine: Overcoming Resistance to Value-Free Development." *Social Problems* 31:484-499.

O'Connor, James. 1973. *The Fiscal Crisis of the State.* New York: St. Martin's Press.

Ottensmeyer, Edward J., Craig R. Humphrey, and Rodney A. Erickson. 1987. "Local Industrial Development Groups: Perspectives and Profiles." *Policy Studies Review* 6:569–583.

Piore, Michael J., and Charles F. Sabel. 1984. *The Second Industrial Divide: Possibilities for Prosperity.* New York: Basic Books.

Rubin, Herbert J. 1986. "Local Economic Development Organizations and Activities of Small Cities in Encouraging Economic Growth." *Policy Studies Journal* 14:363–388.

Rubin, Irene, and Herbert J. Rubin. 1987. "Economic Development Incentives: The Poor (Cities) Pay More." *Urban Affairs Quarterly* 23:37–62.

Rudel, Thomas K. 1989. *Situations and Strategies in American Land-use Planning.* Cambridge: University Press.

Salamon, Lester M. 1987. "Partners in Public Service: The Scope and Theory of Government-Nonprofit Relations." In *Nonprofit Sector. A Research Handbook,* edited by Walter W. Powell, pp. 99–117. New Haven, Conn.: Yale University Press.

———, and Alan Abramson. 1986. *The Non-profit Sector and the New Federal Budget.* Washington, D.C.: Urban Institute Press.

Stone, Clarence N. 1990. *Regime Politics: Governing Atlanta, 1946–1988.* Lawrence: University Press of Kansas.

Trounstine, Philip J., and Terry Christensen. 1982. *Movers and Shakers. The Study of Community Power.* New York: St. Martin's Press.

U.S. Office of Technology Assessment. 1986. *Technology and Structural Unemployment: Reemploying Displaced Adults.* OTA-ITE-250. Washington, D.C.: U.S. Government Printing Office.

Walsh, Edward J. 1988. *Democracy in the Shadows. Citizen Mobilization in the Wake of the Accident at Three Mile Island.* Westport, Conn.: Greenwood Press.

Wardwell, John M. 1980. "Toward a Theory of Urban-Rural Migration in the Developed World." In *New Directions in Urban-Rural Migration: The Population Turnaround in Rural America,* edited by David L. Brown and John M. Wardwell, pp. 71–114. New York: Academic Press.

Westmoreland Community College. 1976. Clippings file on the Volkswagen relocation into Westmoreland County, Penn. Available from the authors.

Wolman, Harold. 1986. "The Reagan Urban Policy and Its Impacts." *Urban Affairs Quarterly* 21:311–335.

_____. 1988. "Local Economic Development Policy: What Explains the Divergence Between Policy Analysis and Political Behavior?" *Journal of Urban Affairs* 10:19–28.

Chapter 10: Assessing the Federal Role in Revitalizing Youngstown, Ohio

Birch, David. 1981. "Who Creates Jobs?" *Public Interest,* Fall.

Buss, Terry F., and F. Stevens Redburn. 1987. "The Politics of Revitalization: Public Subsidies and Private Interests." In *The Future of Winter Cities,* edited by Gary Gappert, pp. 285–296. Beverly Hills, Calif.: Sage.

_____. 1988. *On the Rebound: A Human Service Response to Plant Closings.* Washington, D.C.: Council of State Planning Agencies.

Buss, Terry F., and Roger J. Vaughan. 1987. "Revitalizing the Mahoning Valley." *Environment and Planning: Government and Policy* 5 (1987):433–446.

General Accounting Office (GAO). 1987 (March). *A Catalog of Federal Aid to States and Localities.* Washington, D.C.: GAO.

Lin, Xiannian, Terry F. Buss, and Mark Popovich. 1990. "Entrepreneurship Is Alive and Well in Rural America." *Economic Development Quarterly,* 4:254–259.

Redburn, F. Stevens, and Terry F. Buss. 1984. "Religious Leaders and the Politics of Revitalization." In *Public Policy Formation,* edited by Robert Eyestone. Greenwich, Conn.: JAI Press.

Vaughan, Roger J., and Terry F. Buss. 1988. *Making a Comeback: Local, Long-Term Economic Development Strategies.* Washington, D.C.: Council of State Planning Agencies.

Vaughan, Roger J., Robert Pollard, and Barbara Dyer. 1984. *Wealth of States.* Washington, D.C.: Council of State Planning Agencies.

Chapter 11: Transportation as a Variable in the Site Selection Decisions of Firms

Blakely, Edward J. 1989. *Planning Local Economic Development: Theory and Practice.* Newbury Park, Calif.: Sage Pubn.

Conway Data. 1983. "Development Opportunities for High Tech: A Meeting of the Minds Is in View." *Site Selection Handbook* 28:532–536.

Council of State Governments. 1984. *Forging Links for a Productive Economy: Partnerships among Government, Business and Education.* Lexington, Ky.: Council of State Governments.

Ellenis, M. 1983. "Six Major Trends Affecting Site Selection Decisions to the Year 2000," *Dunn's Business Month* (Nov.):116–130.

Feller, Irwin. 1984. "Political and Administrative Aspects of State High Technology Programs." *Policy Studies Review* 3:460–466.

Hansen, Susan B. 1989. "Targeting in Economic Development: Comparative State Perspectives." *Publius* 19:47–62.

Kansas Department of Economic Development. 1982. *Strategy for the Eighties: High Technology Industrial Development.* Topeka, Kans.: KDED.

Kamieniecki, Sheldon, and Paula Lackie. 1989. "Measuring High-Technology Capacity across the 50 States." Paper presented at the annual meeting of the American Political Science Assn., Atlanta, Georgia, Aug. 30–Sept. 3.

London, M., C. Crandall, and G. W. Seals. 1977. "The Contribution of Job and Leisure Satisfaction to Quality of Life." *Journal of Applied Psychology* 62:328–334.

Luger, Michael I. 1984. "Does North Carolina's High-Tech Development Program Work?" *Journal of the American Planning Association* 50:280–289.

Lynch, A. A. 1973. "Environment and Labor Quality Take Top Priority in Site Selection." *Industrial Development* 142 (March-April):13–15.

MacManus, Susan A. 1985. "Linking State Employment and Training Programs and Economic Development." Paper presented at the annual meeting of the American Political Science Assn., New Orleans, La., Aug. 28–Sept. 1.

Mauro, F., and G. Yago. 1989. "State Government Targeting in Economic Development: The New York Experience." *Publius* 19:63–82.

National Governors' Association, Task Force on Technological Innovation. 1984. "State Initiatives and Federal Policy." Discussion paper for the winter meeting, Washington, D.C., Feb.

Rasmussen, D. W., and L. C. Ledebur. 1983. "The Role of State Economic Development Programs in National Industrial Policy." *Policy Studies Review* 2:750–761.

Rasmussen, D. W., M. Bendick, Jr., and L. C. Ledebur. 1982. "Evaluating State Economic Development Incentives from a Firm's Perspective." *Business Economics* (May):23–29.

Rubin, B. M., and C. K. Zorn. 1985. "Sensible State and Local Economic Development." *Public Administration Review* 45:333–339.

Schmenner, R. W. 1979. "Look Beyond the Obvious in Plant Location." *Harvard Business Review* 57:126–132.

Shannon, J., and B. D. McDowell. 1985. "Interstate Competition for Industry." Paper delivered at the annual meeting of the American Political Science Assn., New Orleans, La., Aug. 29–Sept. 1.

Smilor, R. W., and M. Gill, Jr. 1985. "Hypercompetitiveness Begins with a Firm's Birth." *Economic Developer* (March):4–7.

Smith, Russell L. 1986. "Interdependencies in Urban Economic Development: The Role of Multi-Establishment Corporations." In *Public Policy Across States and Cities,* edited by Dennis R. Judd. New York: JAI Press.

_____. 1985. "States and Communities: Marginal Actors or Partners with Business in Economic Development?" Paper delivered at the annual meeting of the American Political Science Assn., New Orleans, La., Aug. 29–Sept. 1.

Stone, Clarence N. 1984. "City Politics and Economic Development." *Journal of Politics* (Feb.).

Student, K. R. 1976. "Cost vs. Human Values in Plant Location." *Business Horizons* 19 (April):5–14.

U.S. Congress, Joint Economic Committee, Subcommittee on Monetary and Fiscal Policy. 1982. *Location of High Technology Firms and Regional Economic Development: A Staff Study.* Washington, D.C.: U.S. Government Printing Office.

U.S. Congress, Office of Technology Assessment. 1984. *Technology, Innovation, and Regional Economic Development: Encouraging High-Technology Development, Background Paper #2.* OTA-BP-STI-25.

U.S. General Accounting Office, Comptroller General. 1982. *Report to the Congress: Revitalizing Distressed Areas Through Enterprise Zones.* GAO/CED-82-78.

Waugh, William L., Jr., and Deborah M. Waugh. 1988a. "State and Local Government Economic Development Programs and the Site Selection Decisions of Smaller Firms." In *Small Business in a Regulated Economy,* edited by R.J. Judd, W.T. Greenwood, and F.W. Becker. Westport, Conn.: Greenwood Press.

_____. 1988b. "Baiting the Hook: Targeting Economic Development Monies More Effectively." *Public Administration Quarterly* 12:216–235.

_____. 1991. "The Political Economy of Seduction: Promoting Business Relocation and Economic Development in Nonindustrial States." In *Public Policy and Economic Institutions,* edited by M. J. Dubnick and A. Gitelson. Greenwich, Conn.: JAI Press.

Welles, N. 1981. "What Site Selection Consultants Are Saying Now." *Institutional Investor* (Nov.):163–182.

Chapter 12: Organizational Impacts on Firm Location Decisions

Bartik, T. 1988. The Effects of Environmental Regulation on Business Location in the United States." *Growth and Change* 19:22–44.

Beaumont, E., and H. Hovey. 1985. "State, Local and Federal Economic Development Policies: New Federal Patterns, Chaos or What? *Public Administration Review* 45:325–340.

Blair, J., and R. Premus. 1987. "Major factors in Industrial Location: A Review. *Economic Development Quarterly* 1:72–85.

Bozeman, B., and J. Bozeman. 1987. "Manufacturing Firms' View of Government Activity and Commitment to Site: Implications for Business Retention Policy." *Policy Studies Review* 6:538–553.

Carlton, D. 1983. "The Location and Employment Choices of New Firms: An Econometric Model with Discrete and Continuous Endogenous Variables." *Review of Economics and Statistics* 65:440–449.

Charney, A. 1983. "Interurban Manufacturing Location Decisions and Local Tax Differentials." *Journal of Urban Economics* 14:184–205.

Chapman, K., and D. Walker. 1987. *Industrial Location: Principles and Policies.* New York: Basil Blackwell.

Cooper, A. and A. Bruno. 1977. "Success among High-Technology Firms." *Business Horizons* (April):1622.

de Noble, A., and C. Galbraith. 1987. "Criteria for High Technology Location and Development." Paper presented at the annual meeting of the Western Academy of Management, Hollywood, Calif., April.

Denison, D., and S. Hart. 1987. *Revival in the Rust Belt: Tracking the Evolution and Development of an Urban Region.* Ann Arbor: Institute of Social Research, University of Michigan.

Due, J. 1961. "Studies of State-Local Tax Influences on Location of Industry." *National Tax Journal* 14:163–173.

Fox, W. 1981. "Fiscal Differentials and Industrial Location: Some Empirical Evidence." *Urban Studies* 18:105–111.

Galbraith, C. 1985. "High Technology Location and Development: The Case of Orange County." *California Management Review* 28:98–109.

Ghoshal, S. 1987. "Global Strategy: An Organizing Framework." *Strategic Management Journal* 8:425–440.

Grieson, R., W. Hamovitch, A. Levenson, and R. Morgenstern. 1977. "The Effect of Business Tax on the Location of Industry." *Journal of Urban Economics* 4:170–185.

Gorlow, B. 1984. "High-Tech Location Decisions—and Corporate Dynamics." *Urban Land* (Dec.):14–16.

Harding, C. 1988. "Quantifying Abstract Factors in Facility-Locations Decisions." *Industrial Development* 157 (May/June):24–27.

Hart, S., and D. Denison. 1987. "The Creation and Development of New Technology-Based Organizations: A System Dynamics Model." *Policy Studies Review* 6:512–528.

Hart, S., D. Denison, and D. Henderson. 1989. "A Contigency Approach to Firm Location: The Influence of Industrial Sector and Level of Technology." *Policy Studies Journal* 17:599–623.

Hart, S., D. Henderson, and D. Denison. 1989. "The Influence of Age and Size in Industrial Location Preferences." *Academy of Management Proceedings* 1989:307–311.

Hicks, D. 1985. *Advanced Industrial Development: Restructuring, Relocation and Renewal.* Boston, Mass.: Oelgeschlager, Gunn and Hain, with Lincoln Institute of Land Policy.

Hoover, E. 1948. *The Location of Economic Activity.* New York: McGraw-Hill.

Jarboe, K. 1986. Location Decisions of High-Tech Firms: A Case Study. *Technovation* 4:117–129.

Lyne, J. 1988. "Quality-of-Life Factors Dominate Many Facility Location Decisions." *Site Selection Handbook* 33 (Aug.):868–869.

Malecki, E. 1984. "High-Technology and Local Economic Development." *Journal of the American Planning Association* 50:262–269.

_____. 1985. "Industrial Location and Corporate Organizations in High Technology Industries." *Economic Geography* 61:345–369.

_____. 1987. "Hope or Hyperbole? High Tech and Economic Development." *Technology Review* 90 (Oct.):45–51.

Malizia, E. 1985. "The Locational Attractiveness of the Southeast to High-Technology Manufacturers." In *High Hopes for High-Technology: Microelectronics Policy in North Carolina*, edited by D. Whittington, pp. 173–190. Chapel Hill: University of North Carolina Press.

Mandell, L. 1975. *Industrial Location Decisions: Detroit Compared with Atlanta and Chicago*. New York: Praeger.

McDermott, P., and M. Taylor. 1976. "Attitudes, Images and Location: The Subjective Context of Decision Making in New Zealand Manufacturing." *Economic Geography* 52:325–347.

McGuire, T. 1985. "Are Property Taxes Important in the Intra-Metropolitan Location Decisions of Firms? *Journal of Urban Economics* 18:587–592.

McLoughlin, P. 1983. "Community Considerations as Location Attraction Variables for Manufacturing Industry." *Urban Studies* 20:359–363.

Newman, R., and D. Sullivan. 1988. "Econometric Analysis of Business Tax Impacts on Industrial Location: What Do We Know, and How Do We Know It?" *Journal of Urban Economics* 23:215–234.

O'Connor, M. 1987. "Official's Ratings, Local Improvements Underscore Importance of Quality of Life." *Site Selection Handbook* 32 (Aug.):778–784.

Porter, M. 1980. *Competitive Strategy*. New York: Free Press.

Premus, R. 1982. *Location of High Technology Firms and Regional Economic Development*. Washington, D.C.: U.S. Congress Joint Economic Committee, Joint Committee Print.

Rees, J., ed. 1986. *Technology, Regions, and Policy*. Totowa, N.J.: Rowan & Littlefield.

Roberts, E. 1970. "How to Succeed in a New Technology Enterprise." *Technology Review* 73:25–29.

Thwaites, A., and R. Oakey, eds. 1985. *The Regional Economic Impact of Technological Change*. London: Frances Pinter Pub.

Tybout, R., and J. Mattila. 1977. "Agglomeration of Manufacturing in Detroit." *Journal of Regional Science* 17:1–16.

Watts, H. 1987. *Industrial Geography*. London: Longman.

Wasylenko, M. 1980. "Evidence of Fiscal Differentials and Intrametropolitan Firm Relocation." *Land Economics* 56:337–349.

Weiss, J., ed. 1988. *Regional Cultures, Managerial Behavior, and Entrepreneurship*. New York: Quorum Books.

Wiewel, W., J. deBettencourt, and R. Mier. 1982. "Planners, Technology and Economic Growth." *Journal of the American Planning Association* 50:290–296.

Wolman, H. 1988. "Local Economic Development Policy: What Explains the Divergence Between Policy Analysis and Political Behavior?" *Journal of Urban Affairs* 10:19–28.

INDEX